The Chymical Wedding *of* Christian Rosenkreutz

The
Chymical
Wedding
of Christian
Rosenkreutz

A Commentary on a
Christian Path of Initiation

BASTIAAN BAAN

Floris
Books

Commentary translated by Philip Mees

First published in Dutch under the title
De Chymische Bruiloft van Christian Rosencreutz
by Christofoor Publishers, Zeist in 1997
First published in English by Floris Books in 2016

Unless otherwise indicated, Bible quotations are from
the Revised Standard Version
Those marked *M* after the reference are from
The New Testament, a rendering by Jon Madsen,
Floris Books 1994

British Library CIP Data available
ISBN 978-178250-317-0
Printed by TJ International

Contents

Introduction
A Brief History of the Rosicrucians and Their Writings

The Rosicrucians were a secret Christian esoteric order named after its founder, Christian Rosenkreutz. External history is even unclear about whether Christian Rosenkreutz was a real figure, legendary or even merely allegorical. The origins and teachings of the Rosicrucians were described in the anonymous publication in the early seventeenth century of *The Chymical Wedding* and two manifestos, which were all attributed to Johann Valentin Andreae. In subsequent centuries this was followed by a great many writings purporting to be Rosicrucians, some of which appear to show genuine insights.

Built on esoteric truths of the ancient past, the Rosicrucians believed in seeking a spiritual transformation for the benefit of humankind. This transformation was to be achieved not by turning away from the outer world, but by penetrating it to seek its essential nature.

Few spiritual streams in history have caused as much controversy as the Rosicrucians. From the seventeenth century alone, about 1,700 titles of books and pamphlets have been found with reactions for and against so-called "genuine" Rosicrucian writings. Among these are the three books written by Johann Valentin Andreae:

Chymische Hochzeit Christiani Rosencreutz Anno 1459 (The Chymical Wedding). After this had circulated for a number of years in the form of manuscripts, its first printed edition appeared in Strasburg in 1616 (and the first English translation by Ezechiel Foxcroft appeared in 1690);

Fama Fraternitatis oder Brüderschaft des Hochlöblichen Ordens des R. C. An die Häupter, Stände und Gelehrten Europae in 1614 (*A Discovery of the Fraternity of the Most Laudable Order of the Rosy Cross*, first English translation by Thomas Vaughan in 1652);

Confessio Fraternitatis oder Bekenntnis der löblichen Bruderschaft des hochgeehrten Rosencreutzes an die Gelehrten Europae in

1615 (*Confession of the Laudible Fraternity*, first English translation by Thomas Vaughan in 1652). The author of this book is not certain, but it is generally agreed that it originated in the circle of people around Valentin Andreae.*

These books spread like wildfire throughout Europe and brought a movement into existence comparable to the turbulent events of the Reformation. Heated debates raged about them especially in circles of scholars, artists, the nobility and at the courts of rulers.

There may have been no other movement in history that has been opposed more radically than that of the Rosicrucians. Shortly after the appearance of the three books mentioned above it seems as if everyone denounced his opponent as a Rosicrucian. The Lutherans called the Calvinists Rosicrucians, for at that time these two parties fought each other tooth and nail. The Catholics accused the Lutherans of conspiracies under the name of the Rosicrucians. Among the citizenry it was rumoured that the Rosicrucians were a gang of vagabonds. They were supposed to be heretics and sorcerers. A random selection of voices of the time presents some fantastic pictures:

We should set up gallows—that is where these new prophets belong! (*Johannes Sivertus, 1617*)

Christian Rosenkreutz is a village innkeeper soaked in wine ... The Rosicrucians are drunken brothers who only make their secrets known in an inn ... The founder of this godless cabbala believed neither in God nor the devil. (*François Garasse, a Jesuit*)

The Rosicrucians are responsible for the Thirty Years War. (*Christoph Besold, 1659*)

They make fruitless efforts in search of new sciences ... all of this was already done for us in antiquity. (*Andreas Libavius, 1615*)

It did not stop at ideological opposition. History tells us that Adam Haselmayer wrote the first commentary as a reaction to the *Fama*. By order of the Jesuits he was arrested and sentenced to four and a half years of forced labour on a galley. Later Valentin Andreae wrote

---

* A fourth work that is sometimes considered to be one of the "genuine" Rosicrucian writings is *Allgemeine und Generalreformation der ganzen Welt* by the Italian Boccalini; it appeared in German translation in Kassel in 1614.

in his *Turris Babel*: "Shameless comedians have betrayed, corrupted and continued the *Fama*." This makes it understandable that later in his life Andreae radically distanced himself from his youthful writings.

Besides declaring them heretical, people also made the Rosicrucians look like fools. In the course of years, dozens of satires appeared in which well-known people who had consorted with Rosicrucians were ridiculed. The Thirty Years War finished them off. Countless traces and writings of Rosicrucians were then obliterated. Whatever subsequently appeared under the name Rosicrucian had little or nothing to do with the original movement. Some people used the name in order to propagate the exact opposite of the message of the original Rosicrucians. For instance, the English scholar Francis Bacon (1561–1626) adopted elements of Valentin Andreae's ideas and distorted them into materialistic utopias.

For Andreae, the Rosicrucian movement was a matter of community, and it would have to be given form in human society. In 1620 he drew up a plan for a *Societas Christiana*. The Thirty Years War prevented him from carrying out this plan. The historian Karl Heyer (1888–1964) showed in detail how this plan was corrupted by Francis Bacon. In his book *Nova Atlantis* the latter described a utopia of an earthly materialistic paradise ruled by scholars who, as the new initiates, determine what this world will look like, a world based completely on the idea of utility. Only what is useful is good. It seems as if Bacon here described a self-fulfilling prophecy: a world in which it is possible to move underwater in submarines, fly through the air in planes, change climates artificially, and so on.

Also, most of the people who were engaged in Rosicrucianism in later years were no longer able to discern its essence. That is not surprising because of the confusing maze of literature originating from genuine Rosicrucians, charlatans and opponents. For instance, Will-Erich Peuckert (1895–1969), a famous commentator, wrote in the foreword of his book *Die Rosenkreutzer*: "I could not do anything with the things that have been written about the Rosicrucians. I had to write my own history of the Rosicrucians. That took a long time – and I often wondered whether it would not be better to throw the whole thing out the window."

The three books written by Valentin Andreae are, in my opinion, the best sources to arrive at an understanding of what the Rosicrucians really wanted to bring about, and who they were. In my commentaries I make an effort to make the *Chymical Wedding* accessible in our time and to our concepts. On the one hand, anthroposophy, and especially the essay Rudolf Steiner wrote on the *Chymical Wedding*, enables us to engage with this remarkable book.[1]

After having studied this work for many years, I come to the conclusion that it shows in picture language the Rosicrucian path of initiation in four classical steps: Preparation – Offering – Transformation – Communion. In describing the seven-day journey of Christian Rosenkreutz in the *Chymical Wedding* I will try to show this path.

Bastiaan Baan

The translation of the *Chymical Wedding*

The translation of *The Chymical Wedding of Christian Rosenkreutz* in this book was edited from the Foxcroft English edition of 1690 into modern English by Adam McLean and Deirdre Green, and formed the basis of the Magnum Opus Edition, published in 1984. That translation, used by kind permission, has been further revised avoiding archaic words and forms (like "he maketh").

There is a more modern translation by Joscelyn Godwin published in *The Rosicrucian Trilogy* by Weiser, USA in 2016.

The Title Page

Chymische Hoch-
zeit:
Chriſtiani Roſencreütz.
ANNO 1459.

Arcana publicata vileſcunt; & gra-
tiam prophanata amittunt.

Ergo: ne Margaritas obijce porcis, ſeu
Aſino ſubſterne roſas.

Straßburg/
In Verlägung / Lazari Zetzners.
Anno M. DC. XVI.

Commentary on the Title Page

The title page of the first editions of the *Chymical Wedding* shows in Latin the actual nature of the chymical wedding. Without this motto it would be impossible to genuinely engage with the book:

Arcana publicata vilescunt; et gratiam prophanata amittunt.
Ergo: ne Margaritas obiice porcis, seu Asino substerne rosas.
    Secrets revealed lose their value; secrets profaned lose their grace. Hence, throw no pearls before swine, nor strew flowers under asses.

If the secrets in this book would be unravelled, if they would be desecrated, they would lose their value. And it seems as if, in the course of countless attacks on the Rosicrucians and their writings through the centuries, this has actually happened. Opponents have misused the text in all kinds of ways.

The motto is expressed in a different way in the invitation to the wedding, which plays a crucial role on the first day: without purification, catharsis, you cannot connect with the world that is calling you. This is a motif that we can follow through the entire work. It seems self-evident to me that this also holds for the reader who wants to gain access to the *Chymical Wedding*. Catharsis is a necessary prerequisite for making this subject one's own.

We can find this prerequisite notably expressed in Rudolf Steiner's essay on the *Chymical Wedding*. Freely rendered he says: if someone receives an impression of the spiritual world, an imagination, this impression will usually be a riddle to him. We can have the feeling that such an image has much to tell us, but we cannot comprehend or explain it. If we have such an imagination it is better just to observe it for a time and, above all, not to think or try to interpret it.

Anyone who perceives in the spiritual world knows that sometimes imaginations are assigned that to begin with one cannot understand. One must receive them as imaginations and let them ripen within one's soul. As they ripen, they bring forth in one's inner being the power required to understand them. When one tries to explain a vision at the moment it occurs, one usually lacks sufficient power of understanding, and one's thinking becomes distorted. In spiritual experience much depends on having the patience just to make observations – at first simply to accept them, and to wait with understanding them until the right moment arrives.[1]

This also holds true for the contents of the *Chymical Wedding*: we don't need to understand everything right away. We should not even want to! The right way to deal with such images is to live with them and carry them with us for a long time, cherishing them without wanting to analyse them or define them. We can find the latter in many current commentaries.*

The unique aspect of the *Chymical Wedding* is that through the years it offers ever more without giving us the feeling that our search has come to an end, that we have unveiled everything. Perhaps that is the most important characteristic of a genuine spiritual experience, namely that we receive something we most likely cannot really "own" until far into the future.

---

* For instance, in Richard van Dülmen's commentary on the scene of the Second Day in which the barbers shave part of the hair we find the remark, "Sign of purification". But what is completely left out of consideration is the unusual manner in which this takes place, and why the hair is only partly shaved.

The First Day

The First Day

On an evening before Easter Day, I sat at a table, and having (as my custom was) in my humble prayer sufficiently conversed with my Creator, and considered many great mysteries (whereof the Father of Lights his Majesty had shown me not a few) and being now ready to prepare in my heart, together with my dear Paschal lamb, a small, unleavened, undefiled cake; all of a sudden arose so horrible a tempest, that I imagined no other but that through its mighty force, the hill in which my little house was founded would fly into pieces.

But inasmuch as this, and the like from the devil (who had done me many a spite) was no new thing to me, I took courage, and persisted in my meditation, till somebody in an unusual manner touched me on the back; whereupon I was so hugely terrified, that I dared hardly look about me; yet I showed myself as cheerful as (in such occurrences) human frailty would permit. Now the same thing still twitching me several times by the coat, I looked back, and behold it was a fair and glorious lady, whose garments were all sky-coloured, and curiously (like heaven) bespangled with golden stars; in her right hand she bore a trumpet of beaten gold, on which a name was engraved which I could well read but am as yet forbidden to reveal it. In her left hand she had a great bundle of letters of all languages, which she (as I afterwards understood) was to carry to all countries. She also had large and beautiful wings, full of eyes throughout, with which she could mount aloft, and fly swifter than any eagle.

I might perhaps have been able to take further notice of her, but because she stayed so little time with me, and terror and amazement still possessed me, I had to be content. For as soon as I turned about, she turned her letters over and over, and at length drew out a small one, which with great reverence she laid down upon the table, and without giving one word, departed from me. But in her mounting upward, she gave so mighty a blast on her gallant trumpet, that the whole hill echoed from it, and for a full quarter of an hour after, I could hardly hear my own words.

In so unlooked for an adventure I was at a loss how either to advise or to assist my poor self, and therefore fell upon my knees and besought my Creator to permit nothing contrary to my eternal happiness to befall me. Whereupon with fear and trembling, I went to the letter, which was now so heavy, that had it been mere gold it could hardly have been so weighty. Now as I was diligently viewing it, I found a little seal, on which a curious cross with this inscription, IN HOC SIGNO + VINCES [in this sign you will conquer], was engraved.

Now as soon as I espied this sign I was the more comforted, as not being ignorant that such a seal was little acceptable, and much less useful, to the devil. Whereupon I tenderly opened the letter, and within it, in golden letters in an azure field, found the following verses written:

> This day, today
> Is the royal wedding day.
> For this you were born
> And chosen of God for joy
> You may go to the mountain

Whereon three temples stand,
And see there this affair.
Keep watch
Inspect yourself
And should you not bathe thoroughly
The wedding may work your bane.
Bane comes to him who fails here
Let him beware who is too light.

Below was written: SPONSUS ET SPONSA [Bridegroom and Bride].

As soon as I had read this letter, I presently felt faint, all my hair stood on end, and a cold sweat tricked down my whole body. For although I well perceived that this was the appointed wedding of which seven years before I was acquainted in a bodily vision, and which now for so long a time I had with great earnestness awaited, and which lastly, I found so to be by the account and calculation of the planets I had most diligently observed, yet could I never foresee that it must happen under such grievous perilous conditions. For whereas I before imagined that to be a welcome and acceptable guest, I needed only to be ready to appear at the wedding, I was now directed to divine Providence of which until this time I was never certain.

I also found by myself, the more I examined my self, that in my head there was nothing but gross misunderstanding and blindness in mysterious things, so that I was not able to comprehend even those things which lay under my feet, and which I daily conversed with, much less that I should be born to the searching out and understanding of the secrets of nature, since in my opinion nature might everywhere find a more virtuous disciple to whom to entrust her precious, though temporary and changeable, treasures.

I found also that my bodily behaviour and outward good conversation and brotherly love towards my neighbour, were not duly purged and cleansed. Moreover the tickling of the flesh manifested itself, whose affection was bent only to pomp and bravery, and worldly pride, and not to the good of mankind: and I was always contriving how by this art I might in a short time abundantly increase my profit and advantage, rear up stately palaces, make myself an everlasting name in the world, and other similar carnal designs. But the obscure words concerning the three temples particularly afflicted me, which I was not able to make out by any after-speculation, and perhaps should not have done so yet, had they not been wonderfully revealed to me.

Thus stuck between hope and fear, examining myself again and again, and finding only my own frailty and impotence, not being in any way able to succour myself, and exceedingly awe-struck at the event announced, at length I betook myself to my usual and most secure course – after I had finished my earnest and most fervent prayer, I laid myself down in my bed, so that perchance my good angel by the divine permission might appear, and (as it had sometimes formerly happened) instruct me in this doubtful affair. Which to the praise of God, my own good and my neighbours' faithful and hearty warning and amendment, did now likewise come about.

For I had yet scarcely fallen asleep, when I thought that I, together with an innumerable multitude of men, lay fettered with great chains in a dark dungeon in which, without the least glimpse of light, we swarmed like bees one over another, and thus rendered each other's affliction more grievous. But although neither I nor any of the rest could see one jot, yet I continually heard one heaving himself above the other, when his chains and fetters had become ever so slightly lighter, though none of us had much reason to shove up above the other, since we were all captive wretches.

Now when I with the rest had continued a good while in this affliction, and each was still reproaching the other with his blindness and captivity, at length we heard many trumpets sounding together and kettle-drums beating in such a masterly fashion, that it even revived us in our calamity and made us rejoice. During this noise the cover of the dungeon was lifted up from above, and a little light let down to us. Only then could the bustle we kept be truly discerned, for all went pell-mell, and he who perchance had heaved himself up too much, was forced down again under the others' feet. In brief, each one strove to be uppermost. Neither did I myself linger, but with my weighty fetters slipped up from under the rest, and then heaved myself upon a stone, which I laid hold of; however, I was grasped at several times by others, from whom yet as well as I might, I still guarded myself with hands and feet. For we imagined nothing other but that we should all be set at liberty, which yet fell out quite otherwise.

For after the nobles who looked upon us from above through the hole had recreated themselves a while with our struggling and lamenting, a certain hoary-headed ancient man called to us to be quiet, and having scarcely obtained this, began (as I still remember) to speak on thus:

> If the poor human race
> Were not so arrogant
> It would have been given much good
> From my mother's heritage,
> But because the human race will not take heed
> It lies in such straits

And must be held in prison.
And yet my dearest mother
Will not regard their mischief,
She leaves her lovely gifts
That many a man might come to the light,
Though this may chance but seldom
That they be better prized
Nor reckoned as mere fable.

Therefore in honour of the feast
Which we shall hold today,
That her grace may be multiplied
A good work will she do:
The rope will now be lowered
Whoever may hang on to it
He shall be freed.

He had scarcely finished speaking when an ancient matron commanded her servants to let down the cord seven times into the dungeon, and draw up whosoever could hang upon it. Good God! that I could sufficiently describe the hurry and disquiet that then arose amongst us; for everyone strove to get to the cord, and yet only hindered each other. But after seven minutes a sign was given by a little bell, whereupon at the first pull the servants drew up four. At that time I could not get very near the cord, having (as is before mentioned) to my huge misfortune, betaken myself to a stone at the wall of the dungeon; and thereby I was made unable to get to the cord which descended in the middle.

The cord was let down the second time, but many, because their chains were too heavy, and their hands too tender, could not keep their hold on the cord, but with themselves beat down many another who else perhaps might have held fast enough; nay, many a one was forcibly pulled off by another, who yet could not himself get at it, so mutually envious were we even in this our great misery. But they of all others most moved my compassion whose weight was so heavy that they tore their very hands from their bodies, and yet could not get up. Thus it came to pass that at those five times very few were drawn up. For as soon as the sign was given, the servants were so nimble at drawing the cord up, that the most part tumbled one upon another, and the cord, this time especially, was drawn up very empty.

Whereupon the greatest part, and even I myself, despaired of redemption, and called upon God that he would have pity on us, and (if possible) deliver us out of this obscurity; who then also heard some of us. For when the cord came down the sixth time, some of them hung themselves fast upon it; and whilst being drawn up, the cord swung from one side to the other, and (perhaps by the will of God) came to me, and I suddenly caught it, uppermost above all the rest, and so at length beyond hope came out. At which I rejoiced exceedingly, so that I did not perceive the wound which during the drawing up I had received on my head from a sharp stone, until I, with the rest who were released (as was always done before) had to help with the seventh and last pull; at which time through straining, the blood ran down all over my clothes, which I nevertheless because of my joy did not take notice of. Now when the last drawing up on which the most of all hung was finished, the matron caused the cord to be laid aside, and asked her aged son to declare her resolution to the rest of the prisoners, who after he had thought a little spoke thus unto them.

> You children dear
> You who are here,
> It is completed
> What long has been known,
> The great favour which my mother
> Has here shown you twain
> You should not disdain:
> A joyful time shall soon be come.
> When each shall be the other's equal,
> No one be poor or rich,
> And who was given great commands
> Must bring much with him now,
>
> And who was much entrusted with
> Stripped to the skin will be,
> Wherefore leave off your lamentation
> Which is but for a few days.

As soon as he had finished these words, the cover was again put to and locked down, and the trumpets and kettle-drums began afresh, yet the noise of them could not be so loud but that the bitter lamentation of the prisoners which arose in the dungeon was heard above all, which soon also caused my eyes to run over.

Presently afterwards the ancient matron, together with her son, sat down on seats before prepared, and commanded the redeemed should be told. Now as soon as she had demanded everyone's name, which were also written down by a little page; having viewed us all, one after another, she sighed, and spoke to her son, so that I could well hear her, "Ah, how heartily I am grieved for the poor men in the dungeon! I would to God I could release them all."

To which her son replied, "It is, mother, thus ordained by God, against whom we may not contend. If we were all of us lords, and possessed all the goods upon earth, and were seated at table, who would there then be to bring up the service?"

Whereupon his mother held her peace, but soon after she said, "Well, however, let these be freed from their fetters," which was likewise presently done, and I was the last except a few; yet I could not refrain (though I still looked upon the rest) but bowed myself before the ancient matron, and thanked God that through her, he had graciously and fatherly vouchsafed to bring me out of such darkness into the light. After me the rest did likewise, to the satisfaction of the matron.

Lastly, to everyone was given a piece of gold for a remembrance, and to spend by the way, on the one side of which was stamped the rising sun, and on the other (as I remember) these three letters, D.L.S.;* and therewith everyone had license to depart, and was sent to his own business with this annexed limitation, that we to the glory of God should benefit our neighbours, and reserve in silence what we had been entrusted with; which we also promised to do, and so departed one from another. But because of the wounds which the fetters had caused me, I could not well go forward, but halted on both feet, which the matron presently espying, laughing at it, and calling me again to her said thus to me: "My son, do not let this defect afflict you, but call to mind your infirmities, and therewith thank God who has permitted you even in this world, and in your state of imperfection, to come into so high a light; and keep these wounds for my sake."

Whereupon the trumpets began to sound again, which gave me such a shock that I woke up, and then first perceived that it was only a dream, but it so strongly impressed my imagination that I was still perpetually troubled about it, and I thought I still felt the wounds on my feet. However, by all these things I understood well that God had vouchsafed that I should be present at this mysterious and bidden wedding. Wherefore with childlike confidence I returned thanks to his Divine Majesty, and besought him that he would further preserve me in fear of him, that he would daily fill my heart with wisdom and understanding, and at length graciously (without deserting me) conduct me to the desired end. *Great prayer*

Hereupon I prepared myself for the way, put on my white linen coat, girded my loins, with a blood-red ribbon bound cross-ways over my shoulder. In my hat I stuck four red roses, so that I might sooner be noticed amongst the throng by this token. For food I took bread, salt and water, which by the counsel of an understanding person I had at certain times used, not without profit, in similar occurrences.

But before I left my cottage, I first, thus dressed in wedding garment, fell down upon my knees, and besought God that in case such a thing were, he would vouchsafe me a good conclusion. And thereupon in the presence of God I made a vow that if anything through his grace should be revealed to me, I would employ it for neither my own honour nor my own authority in the world, but to the spreading of his name, and in the service of my neighbour. And with this vow, and good hope, I departed out of my cell with joy.

The First Day: Commentary

The first day takes place on an evening before Easter, which appears from the context: Christian Rosenkreutz is preparing a paschal lamb and unleavened bread in his heart. For most of the commentators this means that the story begins on Maundy Thursday. It is interesting to use this view to trace what happens on the second day (Good Friday), the third day (Holy Saturday) and the fourth day (Easter). Something of the qualities of these days is reflected in the first four days of the *Chymical Wedding*.

In the very first sentence we find a key word that is decisive for the further course of events, a word that we shall meet repeatedly: "I sat at a table, and having (as my custom was) in my humble prayer sufficiently conversed with my Creator ..." Apparently it is impossible to step across the threshold of the spiritual world without humility. With every new event, the original edition of 1616 mentions a key word in the margin. In this place it has the word "meditation" in the margin. It indicates that the person is in a certain respect prepared for an encounter with the spiritual world. He reflects – one can also say meditates – on the secrets of the Father; he prepares the paschal lamb, the gift of the Son. A mighty wind suddenly arises: traditionally the sign that the Holy Spirit is working. The image of the Trinity thus stands there at the beginning of the first day, the image that forms the centre of all the works of the Rosicrucians.

The classic motto of the Rosicrucians expresses it with the words:

Ex Deo nascimur
In Christo morimur
Per Spiritum (Sanctum) reviviscimus.

From God we are born
In Christ we die
By the Holy Spirit we come back to life.

The *Fama* relates that these words were found in the little book that Christian Rosenkreutz was holding in his hands when his grave was discovered and opened 120 years after his death.
Christian Rosenkreutz lives in a peculiar dwelling. The story tells us that it is carved out of the rocks. He lives in the earth. This is a

picture that plays an important role with alchemists. They represent themselves as mineworkers in a cave, with the Latin caption *Visita interiora terrae* – visit the interior of the earth (Figure 1). We literally encounter this picture on the third day, when Christian Rosenkreutz enters into a terrestrial globe. In contrast to the medieval mystics, who left the earthly vale of tears behind and united themselves with heaven in their mystical marriage, in the *Chymical Wedding* the striving is for a profound connection with the earth, the material world. The alchemists also sought this connection by using phenomena of the material world, chemical processes, to develop insight into the reality of the spirit. We will return to this at length in the descriptions of the fourth, fifth and sixth days.

A terrible storm suddenly springs up: the spiritual world reveals itself and puts everything in movement – yes, it even causes desperation and fear. As soon as this world reveals itself in the appearance of an angel, the human being feels unworthy and powerless. "Every angel is terrible," said the poet Rainer Maria Rilke. The image of a woman appears, wrapped in a blue cloak spangled with golden stars. Her wings are studded with eyes. We recognise this image from the prophecy of Ezekiel, to whom angels of a lofty hierarchy, the cherubim, appear in this imagination. The picture of the wings with countless eyes shows an all-seeing capacity, an overwhelming consciousness compared with which the little spark of self-consciousness of the human being disappears into nothingness (Ezek.10:12).

The image of the blue cloak with golden stars plays a very important role in the tradition of the Rosicrucians, even in the form of the spaces in which they performed their rituals. Ludwig Polzer-Hoditz, one of Rudolf Steiner's close collaborators, described a remarkable discovery in his castle in Tannbach, Upper Austria. When Rudolf Steiner had spent the night there, he asked his host the next morning: "What kind of space is there under the floor here? May I take a look at it?" Surprised, Polzer-Hoditz took him to the cellar. There Rudolf Steiner called his attention to something he had never noticed in all the years he had lived there. The space was exactly square; the ceiling consisted of a vault with four crossing ribs. Steiner related: "This is a space where Rosicrucians used to work. Look, you can recognise it by the vaulted ceiling. Originally it was blue with golden stars."[1]

The Rosicrucians often chose to work in subterranean spaces. The square surface emphasised the four directions of earthly space, and above them they depicted the vault of heaven. By analogy with the imagination of the *Chymical Wedding*, this created for them a visible and tangible image of an encounter with the spiritual world: heaven and earth touch each other.

Not only does this world become visible as an imagination, it also becomes audible – the trumpet with a sound that cuts to the marrow. Wherever spiritual tradition speaks of a trumpet (as in the Book of Revelation) we meet with inspirations that reverberate even into the physical nature of the world; they shake the world to its foundations.

When Christian Rosenkreutz receives the letter out of the hand of the heavenly messenger he feels completely unworthy, helpless and fearful. There is but one sign that enables the human being to overcome this impotence and weakness: IN HOC SIGNO + VINCES – in this sign you shall overcome. The text of the letter is written in golden letters on blue paper. One could say that it is a miniature of the blue vault of heaven with its golden stars. For people in ancient times, heaven was like a book. In the signs of the stars and planets the old initiates read what was written by the divine world. That is also the original significance of books: in antiquity, books were imprints, as it were, human miniatures of what was written in heaven. That is why the oldest books and letter scripts had an exclusively sacred significance; they did not serve as human means of communication, but as messengers of the divine world.

Besides words, this letter also contains a sign. The alchemists called it Rebis, the sign of the marriage of sun and moon. In this sign sun and moon interpenetrate, and below them is a cross standing on a kind of anchor, a link with the earth. In alchemy this is sometimes called the extended Rosicrucian sign, the sign that connects all antitheses with each other, such as sun and moon, man and woman, earth and heaven. The alchemist Arnaldus de Villanova wrote: "May our mastership be no other than man and wife, and their union."[2]

Before human beings can share in this union of all antitheses they have to subject themselves to thorough self-knowledge: "Keep watch, inspect yourself!" This appeal – know yourself – is invariably the preparation for every initiation. Then follows the well-known motif

Figure 1. Illustration from manuscript Aurora consurgens, *Zentralbibliothek, Zurich*

of catharsis, purification, with the words: "And should you not bathe thoroughly, the wedding may work your bane."

Christian Rosenkreutz has been able to prepare for this event for seven years. In an imagination ("bodily vision") seven years before, he had received the annunciation of this message. Only now does he begin to understand what that meant; his head is in a whirl, he breaks out in a cold sweat. Maybe that is a sign that a spiritual experience is authentic; it generates a profound realisation of impotence and unworthiness. Someone who had experience in these matters, Michael Bauer (1871–1929) once wrote in a letter to his friend Michael Kelber:

> We humans are the youngest, dumbest and most awkward
> children in the line of the hierarchies. The aftertaste of every
> genuine contact with the divine world is far removed from
> everything having to do with pride and self-conceit. When
> that raises its head it can only come from some playful
> meddling with esoterics or dreamy imprisonment in the realm
> of Lucifer.

Against this background the most diverse spiritual "revelations" offered these days by all kinds of people – sometimes literally offered for sale – turn out to be of questionable nature. The hallmark of genuine contact with the spiritual world is rather that a person becomes extremely modest, extremely reticent and extremely humble.

How many "prophets" and "seers" of our time can truthfully say that of themselves? All too often the tear in the prophet's mantle becomes visible sooner or later, followed by bitter disappointment in those who had followed him and held fast to his mantle. This does not mean that everything of this nature is insignificant or harmful; but it does mean that one has to have the discernment to separate the wheat from the chaff.

Self-knowledge and humility are prerequisites for crossing the threshold to the spiritual world. In the Middle Ages, pride was called the greatest obstacle to achieving union with the spiritual world. The great saints practised humility all their lives. A legend tells of Pacificus, one of the brothers of St Francis, that he had a vision in which he saw heaven opened. He saw thrones on which high angel beings were seated. But one throne was empty. When Pacificus asked: "Why is this throne empty? Who is to sit there?" an angel answered: "This throne was once abandoned by Lucifer, and it will be taken by the humblest of all human beings, Francis."

Here, in the most human quality of humility, the great mystics and the Rosicrucians come together. Later we shall see that the paths to their goal – the *Chymical Wedding* and the Mystical Marriage – are very different. The sobering self-knowledge gained on these paths poses a danger that is eloquently described in the *Chymical Wedding*:

> Thus stuck between hope and fear, examining myself again
> and again, and finding only my own frailty and impotence, not
> being in any way able to succour myself, and exceedingly awe-
> struck at the event announced, at length I betook myself to my
> usual and most secure course – after I had finished my earnest
> and most fervent prayer, I laid myself down in my bed ...

Sleep is the perfect means to resolve everything that tends to come to a dead end from which there seems to be no way out. It opens the way to a connection with the guiding powers who are a step ahead of human beings, and who say to us tottering toddlers in the spiritual world: "Take my hand and make a step. Look, that is the way." Thus it is given to Christian Rosenkreutz in his dream to have a preview of the next step on his path. In extremely realistic spiritual pictures this dream shows where the human being stands – "the youngest, dumbest, most awkward children in the line of the hierarchies."

A large number of people are chained in a dark tower. It is the picture of drab everyday existence: "We were all captive wretches." However, when the ceiling is opened and the spiritual world appears and sounds, every one of the captives wants to be first – especially since that world offers to help them. But this help can only be effective when a human being does not try to rise above others. The first words the old man speaks who announces that help is coming are:

> If the poor human race
> Were not so arrogant
> It would have been given much good
> From my mother's heritage,
> But because the human race will not take heed
> It lies in such straits
> And must be held in prison.

The spiritual world has great gifts ("much good") for the human race; only those human beings will receive these who do not strive to rise above others in pride or jealousy ("were not so arrogant"). Only when human beings are able to simply stretch out their hand to God like beggars for the spirit – only then can they actually receive those gifts.

The message is brought by a "hoary-headed ancient man." The actual gift is bestowed by his mother, who undoubtedly must have been even older! Spiritual development is only possible if we connect ourselves with the forces that cause us to age, the forces of death. The forces of life in the human being make it impossible to follow a spiritual path of development; rather, they are an obstacle on that path.

After the announcement by the old man, a rope is let down into the tower seven times. Now things become really bad, for when a human being develops a personal relationship with the spiritual world, envy arises, competition, mutual conflict. Against all odds, Christian Rosenkreutz is one of those who are freed. He is standing on a large stone by the wall of the tower; one could say that he leads the life of a hermit, separate from the crowds of people. Also in the rest of the story, time and again, he is different from the others; he travels a path all his own. Once he is out of the tower it is his turn to help the ones who come after him: those who have developed themselves further, the leaders, have to offer their services to the ones who follow.

When the rope has been pulled up for the last time, the old man's speech includes the following words:

> A joyful time shall soon be come.
> When each shall be the other's equal,
> No one be poor or rich,

This is an expression of the task Rosicrucians set for themselves, namely to create by their work the greatest possible harmony. They derive their social order from the spiritual laws of nature. *Ars Naturae Ministra* (Art is the Servant of Nature) reads the imprint on the gold medal which the Knights of the Golden Stone receive on the seventh day. When we discover the spirit in nature, we also find the principles that can make for a healthy social life. At the same time, this social objective represents an incredibly difficult task for those who achieve a high level of development:

> And who was given great commands
> Must bring much with him now,
> And who was much entrusted with
> Stripped to the skin will be.

Not only is much entrusted to those who are most highly developed, they also receive heavy burdens to bear. The great initiates do not stand like invulnerable Olympians above all human troubles, but they go through the most arduous trials of all. The tradition of the Jewish people says about its greatest initiate, Moses, that he was a much plagued man, more than any other human being on earth.

On the way to initiation, however, every human being will go through a stage of egoism, whether he wants to or not. Without this stage, spiritual development is practically inconceivable. It is tragic, however, that countless forms of spirituality never grow beyond

Figure 2. Illustration from Basilius Valentinus, Twelve Keys.

this stage. In his work *Twelve Keys (Zwölf Schlüssel),* published in 1599, the alchemist Basil Valentine shows four grades of spiritual development in the pictures of the raven, the peacock, the swan and the pelican that burns itself like a phoenix (Figure 2).

In the first stage, the raven, human beings find themselves at the bottom of the tower, chained to the weight of the earth. As soon as they begin to develop as individuals, that is, as soon as the rope is thrown down to them, ambition and ostentatiousness – egoism – begin to play their part: the stage of the peacock. As they continue on the path of initiation, human beings must practice inner purification (the stage of the white swan) culminating finally in a readiness to offer up everything they have achieved: the stage of the pelican of which tradition says that it pecks its breast in order to feed its young with its own blood, and that it burns in its own fire.

The dream of the tower also shows a remarkable way between the one-sidedness of so-called self-redemption and that of passively waiting for the bestowal of grace. One has to wait until the rope comes down, but one must also take hold of it when it is pulled up again! These two spiritual paths have fought each other with their one-sided approaches since time immemorial and continue to do so in our day. The one only knows grace, to which one has to surrender; the other imagines that one can do it all oneself, like a spiritual do-it-yourself exercise.

A priceless expression of the middle way between these extremes is given in a story of Rabbi Nachman, told by Martin Buber in his *Tales of the Hassidim:*

> The souls of human beings descended from heaven to earth
> down a long ladder. The ladder was then removed. And now
> the souls are calling to go back to the land of their birth. Some
> of them do not move – for how can you climb to heaven
> without a ladder? Others jump and fall, jump again and finally
> give up. But there are a few who, although they know very
> well that they cannot reach heaven, nevertheless keep trying
> until, in the end, God seizes them and pulls them up.

When the ceiling is closed again, those who were freed are counted. The old woman looks them in the eye, one by one, and wants to know the name of each. The first requirement to enter heaven is one's own identity, one's own name. This is followed by enigmatic words about those left behind. The woman says: "Ah, how heartily I am grieved for the poor men in the dungeon! I would to God I could release them all."

The son answers her: "It is, mother, thus ordained by God, against whom we may not contend. If we were all of us lords, and possessed all the goods upon earth, and were seated at table, who would there then be to bring up the service?"

The mother falls silent. The spiritual world not only needs highly developed initiates, who possess "all the goods upon earth," it also needs the ones who remain behind in the tower, the "common people," who serve the gods. The divine world cannot do without earthly human beings. Rudolf Steiner expressed this law by saying that our religion, the religion of human beings is the divine. Does God also have a religion? And to this most surprising question he answered that the religion of God is the human being. The divine world looks at the human world with the greatest imaginable longing for connection *(religio)*.

These events of the first day – still in the dream – are affirmed with a gold medal imprinted with the letters D.L.S. What we acquire and make our own is imprinted in our soul. In the 1616 edition, Valentin Andreae interprets this as meaning *Deus Lux Solis* (God is the Light of the Sun) or *Deo Laus Semper* (Praise to God Always). However, we can also listen to the sounds themselves and discern three different worlds in them: the D as a percussive sound that gives solid support, the L as a flowing sound, and the S as a sound that takes flight. Maybe this could be an indication of the qualities of the Trinity: the Father's world that carries us, the world of the Son who brings movement into life, and the Holy Spirit who liberates us.

Viewed from an earthly perspective, Christian Rosenkreutz is a highly developed individual at this stage. In the spiritual world he is clumsy and injured; he has a limp in both legs. Something similar was said of the greatest among humanity, John the Baptist: "Yet he who is least in the kingdom of heaven is greater than he" (Mt.11:11).

When Christian Rosenkreutz wakes up from his dream he dresses himself for a wedding: a white linen coat, a blood-red belt crosswise over the shoulders and a hat with four red roses. Some people recognise in this the family crest of Valentin Andreae, the cross of St Andrew with four roses. However, we can go beyond this outer resemblance. The image of the cross and the roses is far older than this, and it plays an important role in the world of alchemical imagery. As Kossmann says in his dissertation *Alchemie und Mystik:* "The concepts are decisive in their religious and alchemical significance, not because of their appearance in the family crest of Andreae."

The first day ends as it began, with prayer. Christian Rosenkreutz leaves his cell, not to make a name for himself, "but to the spreading of his name, and in the service of my neighbour."

The Second Day

The Second Day

I had hardly got out of my cell into a forest when I thought the whole heaven and all the elements had already trimmed themselves in preparation for this wedding. For even the birds chanted more pleasantly than before, and the young fawns skipped so merrily that they made my heart rejoice, and moved me to sing; wherefore with a loud voice I thus began:

> Rejoice dear bird
> And praise your Maker,
> Raise bright and clear your voice,
> Your God is most exalted,
> Your food he has prepared for you
> To give you in due season.
> So be content therewith,
> Wherefore shall you not be glad,
> Will you arraign your God
> That he has made you bird?
> Will trouble your wee head
> That he made you not a man?
> Be still, he has it well bethought
> And be content therewith.
> What do I then, a worm of earth
> To judge along with God?
> That I in this heaven's storm
> Do wrestle with all art.
> You cannot fight with God.
> And whoso is not fit for this, let him be sped away
> O man, be satisfied
> That he has made you not the king
> And take it not amiss,
> Perchance had you despised his name,
> That were a sorry matter:
> For God has clearer eyes that that
> He looks into your heart,
> You cannot God deceive.

This I sang now from the bottom of my heart throughout the whole forest, so that it resounded from all parts, and the hills repeated my last words, until at length I saw a curious green heath, to which I betook myself out of the forest. Upon this heath stood three lovely tall cedars, which by reason of their breadth afforded excellent and desired shade, at which I greatly rejoiced. For although I had not hitherto gone far, yet my earnest longing made me very faint, whereupon I hastened to the trees to rest a little under them. But as soon as I came somewhat closer, I saw a tablet fastened to one of them, on which (as afterwards I read) in curious letters the following words were written:

God save you, stranger! If you have heard anything concerning the nuptials of the king, consider these words. By us the Bridegroom offers you a choice between four ways, all of which, if you do not sink down in the way, can bring you to his royal court. The first is short but dangerous, and one which will lead you into rocky places, through which it will scarcely be possible to pass. The second is longer, and takes you circuitously; it is plain and easy, if by the help of a compass you turn neither to left nor right. The third is that truly royal way which through various pleasures and pageants of our king, affords you a joyful journey; but this so far has scarcely been allotted to one in a thousand. By the fourth no man shall reach the place, because it is a consuming way, practicable only for incorruptible bodies. Choose now which one you will of the three, and persevere constantly therein, for know whichever you will enter, that is the one destined for you by immutable Fate, nor can you go back in it save at great peril to life. These are the things which we would have you know. But, ho, beware! You know not with how much danger you commit yourself to this way, for if you know yourself to be obnoxious by the smallest fault to the laws of our king, I beseech you, while it is still possible, to return swiftly to your house by the way you came.

As soon as I read this writing all my joy nearly vanished again, and I who before sang merrily, began now inwardly to lament. For although I saw all the three ways before me, and understood that henceforward it was vouchsafed to me to choose one of them, yet it troubled me that if I went the stony and rocky way, I might get a miserable and deadly fall, or if I took the long one, I might wander out of it through byways, or be in other ways detained in the great journey. Neither could I hope that I amongst thousands should be the very one who should choose the royal way. I saw likewise the fourth before me, but it was so environed with fire and exaltations, that I did not dare draw near it by much, and therefore again and again considered whether I should turn back, or take any of the ways before me. I considered well my own unworthiness, but the dream still comforted me that I was delivered out of the tower; and yet I did not dare confidently rely upon a dream; whereupon I was so perplexed in various ways, that very great weariness, hunger and thirst seized me.

Whereupon I presently drew out my bread and cut a slice of it; which a snow-white dove of whom I was not aware, sitting upon the tree, saw, and therewith (perhaps according to her usual manner) came down. She betook herself very familiarly with me, and I willingly imparted my food to her, which she received, and so with her prettiness she again refreshed me a little. But as soon as her enemy, a most black raven, perceived it, he straightaway darted down upon the dove, and taking no notice of me, would force away the dove's food, and she could not guard herself otherwise than by flight.

Whereupon they both flew together towards the south, at which I was so hugely incensed and grieved that without thinking what I did, I hastened after the filthy raven, and so against my will ran into one of the forementioned ways a whole field's length. And thus the raven having been chased away, and the dove delivered, I then first observed what I had inconsiderately done, and that I was already entered into a way, from which under peril of great punishment I could not retire. And though I had still wherewith in some measure to comfort myself, yet that which was worst of all to me was that I had left my bag and bread at the tree, and could never retrieve them. For as soon as I turned myself about, a contrary wind was so strong against me that it was ready to fell me. But if I went forward on the way, I perceived no hindrance at all. From which I could easily conclude that it would cost me my life if I should set myself against the wind, wherefore I patiently took up my cross, got up onto my feet, and resolved, since so it must be, that I would use my utmost endeavour to get to my journey's end before night.

Now although many apparent byways showed themselves, yet I still proceeded with my compass, and would not budge one step from the meridian line; however, the way was often so rugged and impassable, that I was in no little doubt of it. On this way I constantly thought upon the dove and the raven, and yet could not search out the meaning; until at length upon a high hill afar off I saw a stately portal, to which, not regarding how far it was distant both from me and from the way I was on, I hasted, because the sun had already hid himself under the hills, and I could see no abiding place elsewhere; and this truly I ascribe only to God, who might well have permitted me to go forward in this way, and withheld my eyes that so I might have gazed beside this gate.

To this I now made great haste, and reached it in so much daylight as to take a very competent view of it. Now it was an exceedingly royal beautiful portal, on which were carved a multitude of most noble figures and devices, every one of which (as I afterwards learned) had its peculiar signification. Above was fixed a pretty large tablet, with these words, PROCUL HINC, PROCUL ITE PROFANI (keep away, you who are profane), and other things more, that I was earnestly forbidden to relate.

Now as soon as I came under the portal, there straightaway stepped forth one in a sky-coloured habit, whom I saluted in a friendly manner; and though he thankfully returned this salute, yet he instantly demanded of me my letter of invitation. O how glad was I that I had then brought it with me! For how easily might I have forgotten it (as it also chanced to others) as he himself told me! I quickly presented it, wherewith he was not only satisfied, but (at which I much wondered) showed me abundance of respect, saying, "Come in my brother, you are an acceptable guest to me," and entreated me not to withhold my name from him.

Now I having replied that I was a Brother of the Red-Rosy Cross, he both wondered and seemed to rejoice at it, and then proceeded thus: "My brother, have you nothing about you with which to purchase a token?"

I answered that my ability was small, but if he saw anything about me he had a mind to, it was at his service. Now he having requested of me my bottle of water, and I having granted it, he gave me a golden token on which stood no more than these two letters, S.C.,* entreating me that when it stood me in good stead, I would remember him. After which I asked him how many had come in before me, which he also told me, and lastly out of mere friendship gave me a sealed letter to the second porter.

Now having lingered some time with him, the night grew on. Whereupon a great

* The two letters may stand for *Sanctitate Constantia* (constancy by holiness), *Sponsus Charus* (beloved bridegroom), or *Spes Charitas* (hope, charity).

beacon upon the gates was immediately fired, so that if anyone were still upon the way, he might make haste thither. But the way, where it finished at the castle, was enclosed on both sides with walls, and planted with all sorts of excellent fruit trees, and on every third tree on each side lanterns were hung up, in which all the candles were lighted with a glorious touch by a beautiful virgin, dressed in sky-colour, which was so noble and majestic a spectacle that I yet delayed somewhat longer than was requisite. But at length after sufficient information, and an advantageous instruction, I departed in a friendly manner from the first porter.

On the way, I would gladly have known what was written in my letter, yet since I had no reason to mistrust the porter, I forbore my purpose, and so went on the way until I came likewise to the second gate, which though it was very like the other, yet it was adorned with images and mystic significations. On the affixed tablet was DATE ET DABITUR VOBIS (give and it shall be given to you). Under this gate lay a terrible grim lion chained, who as soon as he saw me arose and made at me with great roaring; whereupon the second porter who lay upon a stone of marble woke up, and asked me not to be troubled or afraid, and then drove back the lion; and having received the letter which I gave him with trembling, he read it, and with very great respect said thus to me: "Now welcome in God's name to me the man who for a long time I would gladly have seen."

Meanwhile he also drew out a token and asked me whether I could purchase it. But having nothing else left but my salt, I presented it to him, which he thankfully accepted. Upon this token again stood only two letters, namely, S.M.*

I was just about to enter into discourse with him, when it began to ring in the castle, whereupon the porter counselled me to run, or else all the pains and labour I had hitherto undergone would serve to no purpose, for the lights above were already beginning to be extinguished. Whereupon I went with such haste that I did not heed the porter, I was in such anguish; and truly it was necessary, for I could not run so fast, but that the virgin, after whom all the lights were put out, was at my heels, and I should never have found the way, had she not given me some light with her torch. I was moreover constrained to enter right next to her, and the gate was suddenly clapped to, so that a part of my coat was locked out, which I was verily forced to leave behind me. For neither I, nor they who stood ready without and called at the gate, could prevail with the porter to open it again, but he delivered the keys to the virgin, who took them with her into the court.

Meanwhile I again surveyed the gate, which now appeared so rich that the whole world could not equal it. Just by the door were two columns, on one of which stood a pleasant figure with this inscription, CONGRATULOR (I congratulate). The other, which had its countenance veiled, was sad, and beneath was written, CONDOLEO (I condole). In brief, the inscriptions and figures were so dark and mysterious that the most dextrous man on earth could not have expounded them. But all these (if God permits) I shall before long publish and explain.

Under this gate I was again to give my name, which was this last time written

* The two letters may stand for *Studio Merentes* (by the study of the worthy), *Sponso Mittendus* (to be given to the bridegroom), *Sol Miineralis* (mineral salt), or *Sal Menstrualis* (menstrual salt).

down in a little vellum book, and immediately with the rest despatched to the Lord Bridegroom. It was here where I first received the true guest token, which was somewhat smaller than the former, but yet much heavier. Upon this stood these letters, S.P.N.* Besides this, a new pair of shoes were given me, for the floor of the castle was laid with pure shining marble. My old shoes I was to give away to one of the poor who sat in throngs, although in very good order, under the gate. I then bestowed them upon an old man, after which two pages with as many torches conducted me into a little room.

There they asked me to sit down on a form, which I did, but they, sticking their torches in two holes made in the pavement, departed and thus left me sitting alone. Soon after I heard a noise, but saw nothing, and it proved to be certain men who stumbled in upon me; but since I could see nothing, I had to suffer, and wait to see what they would do with me. But presently perceiving them to be barbers, I entreated them not to jostle me so, for I was content to do whatever they desired; whereupon they quickly let me go, and so one of them (whom I could not yet see) finely and gently cut away the hair round about from the crown of my head, but over my forehead, ears and eyes he permitted my ice-grey locks to hang. In this first encounter (I must confess) I was ready to despair, for inasmuch as some of them shoved me so forcefully, and yet I could see nothing, I could think nothing other but that God for my curiosity had suffered me to fail. Now these invisible barbers carefully gathered up the hair which was cut off, and carried it away with them.

After which the two pages entered again, and heartily laughed at me for being so terrified. But they had scarcely spoken a few words with me when again a little bell began to ring, which (as the pages informed me) was to give notice for assembling. Whereupon they asked me to rise, and through many walks, doors and winding stairs lit my way into a spacious hall. In this room was a great multitude of guests, emperors, kings, princes, and lords, noble and ignoble, rich and poor, and all sorts of people, at which I greatly marvelled, and thought to myself, "Ah, how gross a fool you have been to engage upon this journey with so much bitterness and toil, when (behold) here are even those fellows whom you know well, and yet never had any reason to esteem. They are now all here, and you with all your prayers and supplications have hardly got in at last." This and more the devil at that time injected, while I notwithstanding (as well as I could) directed myself to the issue.

Meanwhile one or other of my acquaintance here and there spoke to me: "Oh Brother Rosencreutz! Are you here too?"

"Yes (my brethren)," I replied, "the grace of God has helped me in too."

At which they raised mighty laughter, looking upon it as ridiculous that there should be need of God in so slight an occasion. Now having demanded each of them concerning his way, and finding that most of them were forced to clamber over the rocks, certain trumpets (none of which we yet saw) began to sound to the table, whereupon they all seated themselves, every one as he judged himself above the rest;

* The letters may stand for *Sponsi praesentandus nuptiis* (to be given at the bridegroom's wedding), or *Salus per naturam* (healing through nature, or salvation through nature).

so that for me and some other sorry fellows there was hardly a little nook left at the lowermost table.

Presently the two pages entered, and one of them said grace in so handsome and excellent a manner, that it made the very heart in my body rejoice. However, certain great guests made but little reckoning of them, but jeered and winked at one another, biting their lips within their hats, and using other similar unseemly gestures. After this, meat was brought in, and although no one could be seen, yet everything was so orderly managed, that it seemed to me as if every guest had his own attendant. Now my artists having somewhat recreated themselves, and the wine having removed a little shame from their hearts, they presently began to vaunt and brag of their abilities. One would prove this, another that, and commonly the most sorry idiots made the loudest noise. Ah, when I call to mind what preternatural and impossible enterprises I then heard, I am still ready to vomit at it. In a word, they never kept in their order, but whenever one rascal here, another there, could insinuate himself in between the nobles, then they pretended to having finished such adventures as neither Samson nor yet Hercules with all their strength could ever have achieved: this one would discharge Atlas of his burden; the other would again draw forth the three-headed Cerberus out of Hell. In brief, every man had his own prate, and yet the greatest lords were so simple that they believed their pretences, and the rogues so audacious, that although one or other of them was here and there rapped over the fingers with a knife, yet they flinched not at it, but when anyone perchance had filched a gold-chain, then they would all hazard for the same.

I saw one who heard the rustling of the heavens. The second could see Plato's ideas. A third could number Democritus's atoms. There were also not a few pretenders to the perpetual motion. Many a one (in my opinion) had good understanding, but assumed too much to himself, to his own destruction. Lastly, there was one also who found it necessary to persuade us out of hand that he saw the servants who attended us, and would have persuaded us as to his contention, had not one of these invisible waiters reached him such a handsome cuff upon his lying muzzle, that not only he, but many more who were by him, became as mute as mice.

But it pleased me most of all, that all those of whom I had any esteem were very quiet in their business, and made no loud cry of it, but acknowledged themselves to be ignorant men, to whom the mysteries of nature were too high, and they themselves much too small. In this tumult I had almost cursed the day when I came here; for I could not behold but with anguish that those lewd vain people were above at the board, but I in so sorry a place could not rest in quiet, one of those rascals scornfully reproaching me for a motley fool.

Now I did not realise that there was still one gate through which we must pass, but imagined that during the whole wedding I was to continue in this scorn, contempt and indignity, which I had yet at no time deserved, either from the Lord Bridegroom or the Bride. And therefore (in my opinion) he should have done well to sort out some other fool than me to come to his wedding. Behold, to such impatience the iniquity of this world reduces simple hearts. But this really was one part of my lameness, of which (as is before mentioned) I dreamed. And truly the longer this clamour lasted, the more it increased. For there were already those who boasted of false and imaginary visions, and would persuade us of palpably lying dreams.

Now there sat by me a very fine quiet man, who often discoursed of excellent matters. At length he said, "Behold, my brother, if anyone should now come who were willing to instruct these blockish people in the right way, would he be heard?"

"No, truly," I replied.

"The world," he said, "is now resolved (whatever comes of it) to be cheated, and cannot abide to give ear to those who intend its good. Do you see that same coxcomb, with what whimsical figures and foolish conceits he allures others to him. There one makes mouths at the people with unheard-of mysterious words. Yet believe me in this, the time is now coming when those shameful disguises shall be plucked off, and all the world shall know what vagabond impostors were concealed behind them. Then perhaps that will be valued which at present is not esteemed."

Whilst he was speaking in this way, and the longer the clamour lasted the worse it was, all of a sudden there began in the hall such excellent and stately music such as I never heard all the days of my life; whereupon everyone held his peace, and waited to see what would become of it. Now in this music there were all the sorts of stringed instruments imaginable, which sounded together in such harmony that I forgot myself, and sat so immovable that those who sat by me were amazed at me; and this lasted nearly half an hour, during which time none of us spoke one word. For as soon as anyone at all was about to open his mouth, he got an unexpected blow, nor did he know where it came from. I thought since we were not permitted to see the musicians, I should have been glad to view just all the instruments they were using. After half an hour this music ceased unexpectedly, and we could neither see or hear anything more.

Presently after, a great noise began before the door of the hall, with sounding and beating of trumpets, shawms and kettle-drums, as majestic as if the Emperor of Rome had been entering; whereupon the door opened by itself, and then the noise of the trumpets was so loud that we were hardly able to endure it. Meanwhile (to my thinking) many thousand small tapers came into the hall, all of which themselves marched in so very exact an order as altogether amazed us, till at last the two aforementioned pages with bright torches entered the hall, lighting the way for a most beautiful virgin, drawn on a gloriously gilded triumphant self-moving throne. It seemed to me that she was the very same who before on the way kindled and put out the lights, and that these attendants of hers were the very same whom she formerly placed at the trees. She was not now as before in sky-colour, but arrayed in a snow-white glittering robe, which sparkled with pure gold, and cast such a lustre that we could not steadily look at it. Both the pages were dressed in the same manner (although somewhat more modestly). As soon as they came into the middle of the hall, and had descended from the throne, all the small tapers made obeisance before her. Whereupon we all stood up from our benches, yet everyone stayed in his own place. Now she having showed to us, and we again to her, all respect and reverence, in a most pleasant tone she began to speak as follows:

The king, my gracious lord
He is not far away,
Nor is his dearest Bride,
Betrothed to him in honour.

They have now with the greatest joy
Beheld your coming hither.
Wherefore especially they would proffer
Their favour to each one of you,
And they desire from their heart's depth
That you at all times fare well,
That you have the coming wedding's joy
Unmixed with others' sorrow.

Hereupon with all her small tapers she courteously bowed again, and soon after began as follows:

You know what in the invitation stands:
No man has been called hither
Who has not got from God already
All gifts most beautiful,
And has himself adorned aright
As well befits him here,
Though some may not believe it,
That anyone so wayward be
That on such hard conditions
Should dare to make appearance
When he has not prepared himself
For this wedding long before.
So now they stand in hope
That you be well furnished with all good things,
Be glad that in such hard times
So many folk be found
But men are yet so forward that
They care not for their boorishness
And thrust themselves in places where
They are not called to be.
Let no knave be smuggled in
No rogue slip in with others.
They will declare right openly
That they a wedding pure will have,
So shall upon the morrow's morn
The artist's scales be set
Wherein each one be weighed
And found what he forgotten has.
Of all the host assembled here
Who trusts him not in this
Let him now stand aside.
And should he bide here longer
Then he will lose all grace and favour
Be trodden underfoot,

> And he whose conscience pricks him
> Shall be left in this hall today
> And by tomorrow he'll be freed
> But let him come hither never again.
> But he who knows what is behind him
> Let him go with his servant
> Who shall attend him to his room
> And there shall rest him for this day,
> For he awaits the scales with praise
> Else will his sleep be mighty hard.
> Let the others make their comfort here
> For he who goes beyond his means
> 'Twere better he had hid away.
> And now the best from each be hoped.

As soon as she had finished saying this, she again made reverence, and sprung cheerfully into her throne, after which the trumpets began to sound again, which yet was not forceful enough to take the grievous sighs away from many. So they conducted her invisibly away again, but most of the small tapers remained in the room, and one of them accompanied each of us.

In such perturbation it is not really possible to express what pensive thoughts and gestures were among us. Yet most of us were resolved to await the scale, and in case things did not work out well, to depart (as they hoped) in peace. I had soon cast up my reckoning, and since my conscience convinced me of all ignorance, and unworthiness, I purposed to stay with the rest in the hall, and chose rather to content myself with the meal I had already taken, than to run the risk of a future repulse. Now after everyone had each been conducted into a chamber (each, as I since understood, into a particular one) by his small taper, there remained nine of us, and among the rest he who discoursed with me at the table too. But although our small tapers did not leave us, yet soon after an hour's time one of the aforementioned pages came in, and, bringing a great bundle of cords with him, first demanded of us whether we had concluded to stay there; when we had affirmed this with sighs, he bound each of us in a particular place, and so went away with our small tapers, and left us poor wretches in darkness.

Then some first began to perceive the imminent danger, and I myself could not refrain from tears. For although we were not forbidden to speak, yet anguish and affliction allowed none of us to utter one word. For the cords were so wonderfully made that none could cut them, much less get them off his feet. Yet this comforted me, that still the future gain of many a one who had now taken himself to rest, would prove very little to his satisfaction. But we by only one night's penance might expiate all our presumption. Till at length in my sorrowful thoughts I fell asleep, during which I had a dream. Now although there is no great matter in it, yet I think it not impertinent to recount it.

I thought I was upon a high mountain, and saw before me a great and large valley. In this valley were gathered together an unspeakable multitude of people, each of which had at his head a thread, by which he hung from heaven; now one hung high, another low, some stood even almost upon the earth. But through the air flew up and down an ancient man, who had in his hand a pair of shears, with which he cut here one's, there another's thread. Now he that was close to the earth was so much more ready, and fell without noise, but when it happened to one of the high ones, he fell so that the earth quaked. To some it came to pass that their thread was so stretched that they came to the earth before the thread was cut. I took pleasure in this tumbling, and it gave my heart joy, when he who had overexalted himself in the air about his wedding got so shameful a fall that it even carried some of his neighbours along with him. In a similar way it also made me rejoice that he who had all this while kept himself near the earth could come down so finely and gently that even the men next to him did not perceive it.

But being now in my highest fit of jollity, I was jogged unawares by one of my fellow captives, upon which I was awakened, and was very much discontented with him. However, I considered my dream, and recounted it to my brother, lying by me on the other side, who was not dissatisfied with it, but hoped that some comfort might be meant by it. In such discourse we spent the remaining part of the night, and with longing awaited the day.

The Second Day: Commentary

In spiritual tradition, Christian Rosenkreutz is called the great initiate of the west. The first document that appears about him – the *Fama* by Valentin Andreae, published in 1614 – relates that he is initiated in the *Liber Mundi*, the Book of the World. He reads the phenomena of nature as if it were a book of which he knows the script.

In addition to a remarkable biography, the *Fama* tells a fairytale-like story about the legacy Christian Rosenkreutz leaves behind: one hundred and twenty years after his death the Rosicrucians who have practised his teaching in silence discover his grave. In a subterranean vault stands an altar; when the altar is opened the body is found in perfect condition, fully intact and without any decomposition. The little book in the hands of the deceased contains a eulogy that begins as follows:

A Grain Buried in the Breast of Jesus. C. Ros. C. sprung from the noble and renowned German family of R. C.; a man admitted into the Mysteries and secrets of heaven and earth through the divine revelations, subtle cogitations and unwearied toil of his life.[1]

The little book ends with the Rosicrucian motto: *"Ex Deo nascimur – In Jesu morimur – Per Spiritum Sanctum reviviscimus."*

Ever since the publication of the *Fama,* Christian Rosenkreutz has been an exceptional figure in the spiritual tradition of the west. What is so exceptional about the *Chymical Wedding* is that it describes this great initiate as a human being in a way that enables us to follow him in his footsteps on his path of initiation. We are able to "look over his shoulder." And it is remarkable how, for instance on the second day, a person is described on his way to initiation who displays all the human feelings with which we are also familiar.

He is not elevated far above everything that is human; he is exuberantly cheerful, he can be profoundly sad, even desperate; he laughs and he weeps, in brief, the whole range of human feelings is there. It is worth the effort to read through the *Chymical Wedding* simply to discover this colourful range. His path of initiation is so special because he goes through all the movements of the human soul, and because he knows from his own experience what people go through; it is because he himself, in order to attain his place as a great initiate, is dragged through the mud. I realise that this expression may sound shocking in this context; in the tradition of alchemy, however, it is appropriate, as we will recognise on the fourth day.

This brings us to an important quality that the Rosicrucians developed in their practice. Unlike mystics – with whom they are often identified – they did not withdraw into their cells in an effort to overcome their all too human emotions by asceticism and mortification. Actually, that is a hopeless task. A German proverb says: "I tried to drown old Adam, but I failed – he can swim." In the schooling of the Rosicrucians all human emotions – even the most problematic ones – receive their place and are cultivated and transformed. Rudolf Steiner mentions in his essay that Rosicrucians must not put their work in service of human impulses and passions, but they should turn these into mediators of the spirit.[2]

There is, however, one weakness Christian Rosenkreutz has largely overcome when he goes on his way. That is pride. Although he is aware of this most dangerous temptation, he does not become its victim. Throughout his journey he remains human through and through. From time to time people laugh at him – he just lets it be. He does injudicious things; sometimes he wants too much or is curious. Together with others he goes through the depths; he walks the "chymical path." The word chymical comes from the Egyptian word *chemet,* which refers to the black mud that remained behind when the Nile had flooded and receded again. Christian Rosenkreutz takes a path that does not exclude the earth and its troubles. His development is a total contrast to that of a stylite, a saint who lived on a pillar. In early Christian times, the latter withdrew into loneliness, mounted a pillar and "prayed himself into heaven" avoiding all human burdens. Christian Rosenkreutz, on the other hand, connects himself from the beginning to the end of his path with the dark earth and with guilty humanity, which he does not abandon.

Directly at the start of the second day we observe two extremes in Christian Rosenkreutz's emotions. He starts out in exuberant joy in the experience of nature in spring. He sings a song with all his heart in which he tells how every creature receives its assigned place in creation, be it as a bird, an emperor or a common human being. Everyone is assigned a place by the being who foresees what is needed. The lyrics contain an appeal to human beings to unite themselves with this order given by nature and destiny:

> What do I then, a worm of earth
> To judge along with God?
> That I in this heaven's storm
> Do wrestle with all art.

That is the last thing Rosicrucians ever want to do: to storm heaven in an effort to take their destiny into their own hands. Whenever we want to liberate ourselves from the laws of nature and destiny, our fight is in vain: God cannot be fought.

Suddenly this exuberant joy turns into deep earnestness, even despair. The extremes are here very close to each other. It is as if the three cedars lead him to this earnestness. The tablet with the announcement of the four paths that lead to the royal wedding clearly indicates that Christian Rosenkreutz has a long, dangerous way to go, no matter which of the paths he chooses. It shows that there is not one single path to salvation; there are several ways that lead to the divine world.[3]

The first path is short and dangerous, full of rocks and cliffs. We might imagine that this path has to do with thinking, which is capable of anticipating events, but may sometimes prematurely jump to conclusions. In our century we are all too familiar with the cliffs on this path of thinking. The second path is like a middle way: "it is plain and easy, if by the help of a compass you turn neither to left nor right." It is a path that can only be taken slowly and patiently. Finally two other paths are described as hardly passable: the royal path and the path that consumes. We can imagine that these paths can only be accomplished by those who have already achieved initiations in the distant past, individuals who have had experience with such paths.

Most Rosicrucians were familiar with the second path. It is a motto that resounds in many ways in Rosicrucian literature: *Festina lente,*

Hurry slowly, with the symbol of the anchor and the fish (Figure 3): the solidity of the anchor and the mobility of the fish.*

" Lento al consiglio, al fatto diligente."

Figure 3. Colophon of the printer Andrea Alciati of Milan, sixteenth century.

Figure 4. Image on the last page of the 1616 edition of the Chymical Wedding.

---

* The motif of slow, gradual development plays a decisive role in the life of the Count of St Germain and his efforts to avert the French Revolution. It is an example of the Rosicrucian movement that he tried to prevent disaster in social life.
An extensive description and documentation can be found in Heyer, *Geschichtsimpulse des Rosenkreutzertum.*

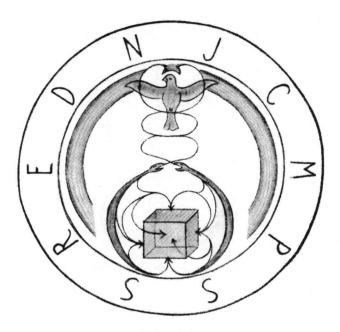

Figure 5. Occult seal by Rudolf Steiner.

The image on the last page of the 1616 edition of the *Chymical Wedding* adds a new element to this picture, which had been known before that time. It shows an upside down anchor on a stone. A serpent that has its head on the stone is twisted around the anchor, while a dove is sitting on the top (Figure 4). On the left and right are the mottos *Simplex Spes* (only hope) and *Prudentia Firma* (firm prudence). Again, a union of great antitheses, hope and prudence. The motif of the Trinity is expressed by the hard stone (the Father Ground that carries life), the anchor with the serpent (the sign of the healer,* the Saviour), and the dove (the Holy Spirit). Rudolf Steiner used this symbol in his own way in one of his occult seals (Figure 5). Around the seal with the cube, the serpent and the dove, are the initials of the Rosicrucian motto: **E**x **D**eo **N**ascimur – **I**n **C**hristo **M**orimur – **P**er **S**piritum **S**anctum **R**eviviscimus.

---

* Compare the pre-Christian sign of the Asclepius.

No matter which path is chosen, "know whichever you will enter, that is the one destined for you by immutable Fate, nor can you go back in it save at great peril to life." The choice is irrevocable.

Christian Rosenkreutz realises that he is not really prepared for any of the four paths. His intellect cannot help him at all in his choice. But then nature comes to his aid in its wondrous way. He feels hungry and thirsty, he eats and drinks – and then unexpectedly he gets help. He shares a piece of his bread with a white dove. As soon as the dove's enemy, the black raven, sees this, it wants to steal the bread. Remarkably, it only desires the bread of the dove, not that of the human being. The creature that has become dark (the black raven) only wants the food that was given to the light creature, the dove. The substance that has been taken up by the good in the human being is the most attractive to the opposing powers. We can recognise this in the lives of the great saints. What they had achieved in prayer and meditation was most desirable for the opposing powers. Hence the trials by demons which play such a large role in the lives of the saints.

The dove flees before the raven, and Christian Rosenkreutz pursues both. Before he knows what he is doing he has chosen his path. Is it really a choice? He had not stopped to think about it. But in this case his legs are wiser than his head, even if they might take him to places where he preferred not to go. "The way chooses you, and you should give thanks," Dag Hammarskjöld wrote in his diary, *Markings*.

How does a human being find the way Providence has marked out for him? Many fairytales, myths, sagas and legends show that intellectual considerations are not the ones that tip the scale; they may even force us into detours. But the moment you turn onto the road you were destined to take is frequently also the time when you momentarily let go of the reins. (In the story of Parsifal this occurs literally: when he is at a loss to find his way to his goal, the Grail Castle, he drops the reins of his horse; the horse then goes its own way and ends up taking him to the castle. It is precisely the moments of total impotence that allow a higher power to take charge.)

Christian Rosenkreutz goes his way, the way that is his. Even when his intellect tells him to return – for he had left his bag and his bread behind by the trees – there is no going back: a violent wind meets him.

He realises that "it would cost me my life if I should set myself against the wind."

In the meantime it is not at all clear which of the four ways he has taken. The use of the compass indicates the second one, but since the path was also "rough and unkept" it reminds us also of the first path that is "short but perilous." Moreover, the portal that he sees standing on a high mountain takes him far from his original path. Finally, the royal building that he arrives at makes us think of the third, the royal path.

Those who do not cling tenaciously to the "prescribed" way that has been traced out for them find their destination. Thus, after a long life in which he had become wise through bitter experience, Goethe was able to write: "The detour was the way." Despite all the detours we have followed, in the end we find our own destiny.

The sign on the royal building is the first thing in the story that literally indicates that a path of initiation is awaiting Christian Rosenkreutz: *Procul hinc, procul ite prophani* (Away, away from here, profane ones). From the words of the porter who welcomes him, it appears that he is on an extraordinary path toward initiation. It is as if this guardian at the threshold recognises him: He "showed me abundance of respect, saying, 'Come in my brother, you are an acceptable guest to me'." When the porter asks him for his name, Christian Rosenkreutz replies that he is a brother of the Rose Cross. They call each other brothers. The porter is like a double, a part of himself. A person who was dying once indicated this deep connection with the double in the words: "Last night I saw my dark twin brother." When someone is about to die, such experiences with the double occur relatively frequently. But also in an initiation, a person has to go through this experience in full consciousness. Christian Rosenkreutz has a most unusual connection with this porter – and the porter with him. He will meet his "twin brother" again on the last day, and then it will become clear how profoundly these two are connected with each other.

At this portal, Christian Rosenkreutz has to leave his bottle of water behind. Every time he has made progress on the path of initiation, he has to leave behind something of himself, something he has made his own. He also receives something new; every step on this path is "confirmed" with a golden memento. In the realm of the spirit something is indelibly engraved. Here it is two sharp, bright sounds that accompany him: the *S,* the sound of the conscious, wakeful spirit, and the light, sharp sound *C.* Andreae adds as possible meanings: *Sanctitate Constantia, Sponsus Charus,* or *Spes Charitas* (constant in holiness, beloved bridegroom or husband, hope, charity). The fact that it is of lasting significance is indicated by the advice of the porter to keep this token in mind.

He then receives a sealed letter for the next porter and continues on his way. However, he lets himself be delayed longer than necessary by a virgin who lights lanterns on the trees. Christian Rosenkreutz is certainly not the quickest on this path; he likes to take his time, also for less serious events.

The next portal bears the sign: "Give and it shall be given to you," a text from the Gospel of Luke (6:38). Here a terrifying lion is keeping watch. When we enter the spiritual world, when the forces that have been "wrapped up" in our body for our entire life come apart, forces that are not yet human are also freed. They are part of every path of initiation. When Dante in his Divine Comedy enters the world of the spirit, he first encounters monstrous animal forms that want to bar his way: a lynx, a lion and a wolf.

Here on earth, of course, we call ourselves human beings, but the moment we step across the threshold of the spiritual world, that is not so certain. Part of us is still animal-like. There are gigantic sub-human forces that slumber in every human being – also in the most civilised ones – and the moment we give them free rein they can do their destructive work.

One person is able to restrain the lion and control him: the porter. He "drove back the lion; and having received the letter which I gave him with trembling, he read it, and with very great respect said thus to me: 'Now welcome in God's name to me the man who for a long time I would gladly have seen'." Would the porter also have said this to the ones who preceded him? I don't think so. Christian Rosenkreutz has a most unusual connection with the two porters – and the porters with him.

He leaves behind the last of his possessions, the salt; he literally has nothing left. The letters on the token that he receives here are: S.M. The sound *S,* the magical sound, returns several times. Here, at the middle portal, is added the sound *M,* which expresses a mediating quality. Andreae adds: *Studio Merentis, Sponso Mittendus, Sal Mineralis,* or *Sal Menstrualis* (by the study of the worthy, pledge for the bridegroom, mineral salt, menstrual salt).

Christian Rosenkreutz has been so slow that he hardly makes it through the third portal, aided by the virgin who lit his way. She will be of great significance to him on his future path. At the gate he leaves behind a piece of his mantle that gets caught in the doors. In our lives on earth we are enveloped in a material mantle. We also have other, invisible mantles, pieces of which we successively have to leave behind, one after another, when we pass through the portals of the spiritual world.

Just as the second day began with two extremes – exuberant joy and deep despair – by this third portal stand two statues that in a certain way display these extremes. A cheerful statue with the inscription *Congratulator;* and the other with a sad expression, *Condoleo.* This is what happens when one crosses the threshold. On the one hand one is congratulated: you made it! On the other hand, one hears condolences, for now the difficulties are just beginning. Between these two extremes – and from his own experience he is all too familiar with them – he has to find his way. He has to go through them; the statues stand there as guardians, on either side.

When he enters, his name is written in a little book; without their own individual name, no mortals may enter here. Thus Christ says of the disciples that their "names are written in heaven" (Lk. 10:20). The third token, the "proper guest token," bears the letters S.P.N: *Salus per Naturam* or *Sponsi Praesentandus Nuptiis* (salvation through nature, to be presented to the Bridegroom at the wedding). The sounds of *P* and *N,* which are new, indicate something that is freed; when we speak, they literally loosen themselves from the lips, to sound in space. Someone who in his profession of eurythmist had worked a great deal with sounds characterised the sound *P* once as follows: "I clothe myself – and display myself." That is so remarkable with everything Christian Rosenkreutz loses: the more he leaves behind, the more he becomes himself!

When he leaves his old shoes behind – and is permitted to give them to one of the beggars at the gate – new shoes replace them. When I related this picture during a course on the *Chymical Wedding,* one of the participants said that he suddenly understood what a dying person had wanted to tell him. While no one understood what he meant, the dying person kept saying: "Look, there are new shoes waiting for me. Just look!" When we are at the end of our life, we are allowed to leave something of the old karma behind and set out on a new path. In this case the old shoes are for the old beggar: like seeks like.

He has hardly arrived in his new surroundings when Christian Rosenkreutz is seized from behind. Barbers "finely and gently cut away the hair round about from the crown of my head, but over my forehead, ears and eyes he permitted my ice-grey locks to hang." Then two pages laugh heartily at him. While we have the tendency to put people who are ahead of us in their development on a pedestal, the spiritual world judges differently, and laughs at our silliness!

Tradition tells us that long hair belongs to a particular religious path. For instance, the Old Testament describes that the members of the Order of the Nazirites wore their hair long. Samson is the well-known example, of whom it was said that his strength lay in his hair. When his hair was cut off he lost his strength. An age-old form of spirituality is connected with this way of wearing the hair.[4] When this form had to be relinquished the head was shaved. Thus the spiritual guidance of Elijah (called "a hairy man" in the Old Testament) is succeeded by the prophet Elisha, who is jeered by children for his bald head.

Christian Rosenkreutz's hair is shaved off on the sides and on the back; only the hair in front is left. Again, an eloquent picture of the old that he has to leave behind.

In the great hall into which he then enters a large crowd of all ranks and classes is assembled. Christian Rosenkreutz is astonished that here, at this stage, all those people, "noble and ignoble, rich and poor," have come in. Later on this will be different; he who has entered last and does not think much of himself will, in the end, be the first. He does not follow his own ambitions: "the grace of God has helped me in too." For those who are trying to "redeem themselves" it seems to be a joke that he would need God's help on this path; people laugh at him again and mock him.

Most of the guests went the short, quick way over the rocks, the way of the intellect. It was abundantly apparent from their bravado and shameless behaviour that in the process other human qualities fell short. "Many a one (in my opinion) had good understanding, but assumed too much to himself, to his own destruction." Those who enter the spiritual world without sufficient preparation will lack the qualities of truthfulness and self-knowledge. While they proclaim their self-conceit and lies with a lot of grandiosity, the sincere seekers for truth keep quiet; they regarded "the mysteries of nature ... too high, and they themselves much too small." They are always aware of their place relative to the invisible helpers who bring them food and drink. Self-knowledge is an absolute prerequisite for making progress. And while on earth the lie can still reign supreme with impunity, in the spiritual world it is silenced. When one of the braggarts goes too far, contending that he can see the servants, he experiences it to his cost: "one of these invisible waiters reached him such a handsome cuff upon his lying muzzle, that not only he, but many more who were by him, became as mute as mice."

Finally, even the biggest braggarts keep quiet. They are forced to, for the world in which they find themselves intervenes immediately when they cross the line. Here on earth people may play the hypocrite and deceive others all their lives. "The world ... is now resolved (whatever comes of it) to be cheated, and cannot abide to give ear to those who intend its good," says Christian Rosenkreutz's quiet neighbour at the table. It is a song we can sing in our time too. But in the spiritual world such excesses receive an immediate reply: evil chastises itself, the lie defeats itself.

The *Chymical Wedding* has been compared with the royal wedding in the Gospel of Matthew. This comparison does not quite work, but the motif of dignity is certainly recognisable. For at the royal wedding only people who are wearing a wedding robe are admitted. At the time when this parable was written the guests at a wedding received a special robe when they came in. The point was that one had to cover oneself – one had to make oneself receptive for the gift of Christ which envelops one like a robe, in the sense of St Paul's words: "Put on the Lord Jesus Christ" (Rom. 13:14).

Preceded by music of kettle-drums, trombones and trumpets and in a sea of living lights, a virgin now enters the hall. It is the same virgin who had shown Christian Rosenkreutz the way before he came to the third portal. She announces that the guests have now arrived in the proximity of the king and his bride. At this time, she continues, it is of the greatest importance not to go against one's destiny but to accept it. And she asks whether everyone who has come has prepared himself for the wedding. Without purification it is not possible to witness it. On the first day already the invitation said: "And should you not bathe thoroughly the wedding may work your bane." An intruder would not only cause confusion for the bride and bridegroom, who want a "pure wedding," but the intruder himself would incur damaging consequences by participating in the wedding. In the spiritual world there is a ubiquitous law: like recognises like.

Now the virgin announces that the next day everyone will be weighed; those who are found to be too light are to be judged.

Once again the guests are presented with a choice: they may choose where they want to sleep. Those who do not have a clear conscience have to spend the night in the hall. Those who think they have nothing to fear are taken to their sleeping quarters by their own little light. Of course, Christian Rosenkreutz, in his modesty and painful self-knowledge, remains behind in the hall. He dares not intrude into a place of which he does not feel worthy. Here again we can recognise the "slow path" that step by little step he makes his own.

Only nine guests remain behind in the hall. To make matters worse, they are all bound in their own spot and left in the dark. At this stage he has to go through the path of absolute, but self-chosen, powerlessness. He chooses not to accept service, but to be the least. It is exactly the Christian disposition indicated by St Paul with the enigmatic words: "I will all the more gladly boast of my weaknesses ... for when I am weak, then I am strong" (2Cor.12:9f). Thoroughly living through the experience of human frailty and powerlessness, is the necessary condition for becoming receptive to the gift that comes to meet him from this world.

The dream with which the second day ends confirms him in this view. It seems to be the counter-image of the first dream. While the dream of the tower was about trying to climb as high as possible out of the chained multitude in order to be pulled up by the rope, now it is about staying close to the earth.

I thought I was upon a high mountain, and saw before me a great and large valley. In this valley were gathered together an unspeakable multitude of people, each of which had at his head a thread, by which he hung from heaven; now one hung high, another low, some stood even almost upon the earth. But through the air flew up and down an ancient man, who had in his hand a pair of shears, with which he cut here one's, there another's thread. Now he that was close to the earth was so much more ready, and fell without noise, but when it happened to one of the high ones, he fell so that the earth quaked. To some it came to pass that their thread was so stretched that they came to the earth before the thread was cut. I took pleasure in this tumbling, and it gave my heart joy, when he who had overexalted himself in the air about his wedding got so shameful a fall that it even carried some of his neighbours along with him. In a similar way it also made me rejoice that he who had all this while kept himself near the earth could come down so finely and gently that even the men next to him did not perceive it.

At this stage of the path of initiation it is more than ever necessary to stay close to the earth, not to have one's head in the clouds, but to practise modesty.

Readers of the *Chymical Wedding* are often surprised because malicious glee and mockery so frequently occur in the story. How does that fit into the seriousness of an initiation? The usual commentaries often put down the *Chymical Wedding* as a mockery.* But those who have experienced what takes place when consciousness frees itself from the body, know that they begin to observe themselves with different eyes, and that they are being observed by the spiritual world. Even in daily life we are familiar with an experience that in some ways may be compared with this: when we are capable of looking at ourselves "over our shoulder," so as to observe ourselves in our actions, we may well laugh at ourselves when we see what we are trying to do. A refreshing and sometimes comic experience!

---

* Valentin Andreae himself, later in life, called his youthful work a joke. Several authors suspect that he was compelled to do so after his opponents had condemned his work as heresy, and because pseudo-alchemists had mutilated the original intentions of his work. See Heyer, *Geschichtsimpulse des Rosenkreuzertums.*

The Third Day

The Third Day

Now as soon as the lovely day was broken, and the bright sun, having raised himself above the hills, had again took himself to his appointed office in the high heaven, my good champions began to rise out of their beds, and leisurely to make themselves ready for the inquisition. Whereupon, one after another, they came again into the hall, and saying good morning, demanded how we had slept that night; and having seen our bonds, there were some that reproved us for being so cowardly, and because we had not, rather, like them, hazarded upon all adventures. However, some of them whose hearts still smote them made no loud cry of the business. We excused ourselves with our ignorance, hoping we should now soon be set at liberty, and learn wisdom by this disgrace, that they on the contrary had not yet altogether escaped; and perhaps their greatest danger was still to come.

At length everyone being assembled again, the trumpets began again to sound and the kettle-drums to beat as formerly, and we then imagined nothing other but that the Bridegroom was ready to present himself; which nevertheless was a huge mistake. For it was again the virgin of yesterday, who had arrayed herself all in red velvet, and girded herself with a white scarf. On her head she had a green wreath of laurel, which greatly suited her. Her train was now no more of small tapers, but consisted of two hundred men in armour, who were all (like her) clothed in red and white.

Now as soon as they were alighted from the throne, she came straight to us prisoners, and after she had saluted us, she said in few words: "That some of you have been aware of your wretched condition is hugely pleasing to my most mighty Lord, and he is also resolved you shall fare the better for it."

And having seen me in my habit, she laughed and said, "Goodness! Have you also submitted yourself to the yoke? I imagined you would have made yourself very smug." With which words she caused my eyes to run over. After which she commanded that we should be unbound, and coupled together and placed in a station where we might easily see the scales. For, she said, it may yet fare better with them, than with the presumptuous who still stand here at liberty.

Meanwhile the scales, which were entirely of gold, were hung up in the middle of the hall; there was also a little table covered with red velvet, and seven weights placed on it. First of all there was a pretty big one, next four little ones, lastly two great ones. And these weights were so heavy in proportion to their bulk, that no man can believe or comprehend it. But each of the armoured men had, together with a naked sword, a strong rope; these she distributed according to the number of weights into seven bands, and out of every band chose one for their own weight; and then again sprang up into her high throne. Now as soon as she had made her reverence, in a very shrill tone she began to speak as follows:

> Whoever goes into an artist's room
> And nothing knows of painting
> And yet will speak with much display
> Will yet be mocked by everyone.
> And he who enters artist's orders
> Who has not been selected

And begins to paint with much display
Will yet be mocked by everyone.
And who will to a wedding come
And has not bidden been,
And yet doth come with much display
Will yet be mocked by everyone.
And who will climb upon these scales
And find he weighs not,
But is shot up with mighty crash
Will yet be mocked by everyone.

As soon as the virgin had finished speaking, one of the pages commanded each one to place himself according to his order, and one after another to step in. Which one of the emperors made no scruple of, but first of all bowed himself a little towards the virgin, and afterwards in all his stately attire went up: whereupon each captain put in his weight, against which (to the wonder of all) he held out. But the last was too heavy for him, so that he must go forth; and that he did with so much anguish that (as it seemed to me) the virgin herself had pity on him, and beckoned to her people to hold their peace; yet the good emperor was bound and delivered over to the Sixth Band. Next after him again there came another emperor, who stepped haughtily into the scale, and, having a great thick book under his gown, he imagined he would not fail; but he was scarcely able to abide the third weight, and was unmercifully flung down, and his book in that upheaval fell from him, and all the soldiers began to laugh, and he was delivered up bound to the Third Band. Thus it went also with some of the other emperors, who were all shamefully laughed at and put in captivity. After these there came forth a short little man with a curled brown beard, also an emperor, who after the usual reverence got up, and held out so steadfastly, that I thought that had there been more weights ready he would have outstood them. To him the virgin immediately arose, and bowed before him, making him put on a gown of red velvet, and finally gave him a branch of laurel, of which she had a good store upon her throne, and bade him sit upon its steps. Now how it fared with the rest of the emperors, kings and lords after him, would take too long to recount; but I cannot leave unmentioned that few of those great personages held out. However, various eminent virtues (beyond my hopes) were found in many. One could stand out this, the second another, some two, some three, four or five, but few could attain to the just perfection; and everyone who failed was miserably laughed at by the bands.

After the inquisition had also passed over the gentry, the learned, and unlearned, and all the rest, and in each condition perhaps one, it may be two, but for the most part none, was found perfect, it came at length to those honest gentlemen the vagabond cheaters, and rascally charlatans, who were set upon the scale with such scorn that I myself, in spite of all my grief, was ready to burst my belly with laughing, nor could the very prisoners themselves refrain. For the most part they could not abide that severe trial, but were jerked out of the scale with whips and scourges, and led to the other prisoners, but to a suitable band. Thus of so great a throng so few remained, that I am ashamed to reveal their number. However, there were persons of quality also amongst them, who notwithstanding were (like the rest) honoured with velvet robes and wreaths of laurel.

The inquisition being completely finished, and none but we poor coupled hounds standing aside, at length one of the captains stepped forth, and said, "Gracious Madam, if it please your Ladyship, let these poor men who acknowledged their misunderstanding be set upon the scale too, without their incurring any danger of penalty, and only for recreation's sake, if perhaps anything that is right may be found amongst them."

In the first place I was in great perplexity, for in my anguish this was my only comfort, that I was not to stand in such ignominy, or to be lashed out of the scale. For I did not doubt that many of the prisoners wished that they had stayed ten nights with us in the hall. Yet since the virgin consented, so it must be, and we were untied and one after another set up. Now although the most part miscarried, they were neither laughed at, nor scourged, but peaceably placed on one side. My companion was the fifth, and he held out bravely, whereupon all, but especially the captain who made the request for us, applauded him, and the virgin showed him the usual respect. After him again two more were dispatched in an instant. But I was the eighth.

Now as soon as (with trembling) I stepped up, my companion who already sat by in his velvet looked kindly upon me, and the virgin herself smiled a little. But for as much as I outstood all the weights, the virgin commanded them to draw me up by force, wherefore three men also hung on the other side of the beam, and yet nothing could prevail. Whereupon one of the pages immediately stood up, and cried out exceedingly loud, *"That is he."*

Upon which the other replied, "Then let him gain his liberty," which the virgin accorded.

And, being received with due ceremonies, the choice was given me to release one of the captives, whosoever I pleased; whereupon I made no long deliberation, but elected the first emperor whom I had long pitied, who was immediately set free, and with all respect seated amongst us.

Now the last being set up, and the weights proving too heavy for him, in the meantime the virgin had spotted my roses, which I had taken out of my hat into my hands, and thereupon presently through her page graciously requested them of me, and I readily sent them to her.

And so this first act was finished about ten in the morning. Whereupon the trumpets began to sound again, which nevertheless we could not as yet see. Meantime the bands were to step aside with their prisoners, and await the judgment. After which a council of the seven captains and us was set, and the business was propounded by the virgin as president, who desired each one to give his opinion how the prisoners were to be dealt with. The first opinion was that they should all be put to death, yet one more severely than another, namely those who had presumptuously intruded themselves contrary to the express conditions. Others would have them kept close prisoners. Both of which pleased neither the president, nor me. At length by one of the emperors (the same whom I had freed), my companion, and myself, the affair was brought to this point: that first of all the principal lords should with a fitting respect be led out of the castle; others might be carried out somewhat more scornfully. These would be stripped, and caused to run out naked; the fourth should be hunted out with rods, whips or dogs. Those who the day before willingly surrendered themselves, might be allowed to depart without any blame. And last of all those presumptuous ones, and they who behaved themselves so unseemly at dinner the day before, should be punished in body and life according to each man's demerit. This opinion pleased the virgin well, and obtained the upper hand. There was moreover another dinner vouchsafed them, which they were soon told about. But the execution was deferred till twelve noon.

Herewith the senate arose, and the virgin also, together with her attendants, returned to her usual quarter. But the uppermost table in the room was allotted to us, they requesting us to take it in good part until the business was fully dispatched. And then we should be conducted to the Lord Bridegroom and the Bride, with which we were at present well content. Meanwhile the prisoners were again brought into the hall, and each man seated according to his quality. They were likewise told to behave themselves somewhat more civilly than they had done the day before, about which they yet did not need to have been admonished, for without this, they had already put up their pipes.

And this I can boldly say, not with flattery, but in the love of truth, that commonly those persons who were of the highest rank best understood how to behave themselves in so unexpected a misfortune. Their treatment was but indifferent, yet respectful; neither could they yet see their attendants, but to us they were visible, at which I was exceedingly joyful. Now although fortune had exalted us, yet we did not take upon us more than the rest, advising them to be of good cheer, the event would not be so bad. Now although they would gladly have us reveal their sentence, yet we were so deeply obligated that none of us dared open his mouth about it.

Nevertheless we comforted them as well as we could, drinking with them to see if the wine might make them any more cheerful. Our table was covered with red velvet, beset with drinking cups of pure silver and gold, which the rest could not behold without amazement and very great anguish. But before we had seated ourselves, in came the two pages, presenting everyone on the Bridegroom's behalf with a golden fleece with a flying lion, requesting us to wear them at the table, and as became us, to observe the reputation and dignity of the order which his majesty had now vouchsafed us; and we should be ratified with suitable ceremonies. This we received with profoundest submission, promising obediently to perform whatsoever his majesty should please. Besides these, the noble page had a schedule in which we were set down in order. And for my part I should not otherwise wish to conceal my place, if perhaps it might not be interpreted as pride in me, which is expressly against the fourth weight.

Now because our entertainment was exceedingly stately, we demanded of one of the pages whether we might not have leave to send some choice bit to our friends and acquaintances; he made no difficulty of it, and everyone sent plentifully to his acquaintances by the waiters, although they saw none of them; and because they did not know where it came from, I myself wished to carry something to one of them. But as soon as I had risen, one of the waiters was at my elbow, saying he desired me to take friendly warning, for if one of the pages had seen it, it would have come to the king's ear, who would certainly have taken it amiss of me; but since none had observed it but himself, he did not intend to betray me, but that I ought for the time to come to have better regard for the dignity of the order. With which words the servant really astonished me so much that for a long time afterwards I scarcely moved in my seat, yet I returned him thanks for his faithful warning, as well as I was able in my haste and fear.

Soon after, the drums began to beat again, to which we were already accustomed: for we knew well it was the virgin, so we prepared ourselves to receive her; she was now coming in with her usual train, upon her high seat, one of the pages bearing before her a very tall goblet of gold, and the other a patent in parchment. Having alighted from the seat in a marvellous skilful manner, she took the goblet from the page, and presented the same on the king's behalf, saying that it was brought from his majesty, and that in honour of him we should cause it to go round. Upon the cover of this goblet stood fortune curiously cast in gold, who had in her hand a red flying ensign, because of which I drunk somewhat more sadly, having been all too well acquainted with fortune's waywardness. But the virgin, like us, was adorned with the golden fleece and lion, from which I observed that perhaps she was the president of the order. So we asked of her how the order might be named. She answered that it was not yet the right time to reveal this, till the affair with the prisoners was dispatched. And therefore their eyes were still veiled; and what had hitherto happened to us, was to them only like an offence and scandal, although it was to be accounted as nothing in regard to the honour that attended us. Hereupon she began to distinguish the patent which the other page held into two different parts, out of which about this much was read before the first company:

"That they should confess that they had too lightly given credit to false fictitious books, had assumed too much to themselves, and so come into this castle, although they were never invited into it, and perhaps the most part had presented themselves with design to make their market here, and afterwards to live in greater pride and lordliness; and thus one had seduced another, and plunged him into this disgrace and ignominy, wherefore they were deservedly to be soundly punished."

Which they with great humility readily acknowledged, and gave their hands upon it. After which a severe check was given to the rest, much to this purpose:

"That they very well knew, and were in their consciences convinced, that they had forged false fictitious books, had fooled others, and cheated them, and thereby had diminished regal dignity amongst all. They knew likewise what ungodly deceitful figures they had made use of, in so much as they spared not even the divine Trinity, but accustomed themselves to cheat people all the country over. It was also now as clear as day with what practices they had endeavoured to ensnare the true guests, and introduce the ignorant: in such a manner that it was manifest to all the world that they wallowed in open whoredom, adultery, gluttony, and other uncleanliness: All which was against the express orders of our kingdom. In brief, they knew they had disparaged kingly majesty, even amongst the common sort, and therefore they should confess themselves to be manifest convicted vagabond-cheaters, knaves and rascals, whereby they deserved to be kept from the company of civil people, and severely punished."

The good artists were loath to come to this confession, but inasmuch as not only the virgin herself threatened them, and swore that they would die, but the other party also vehemently raged at them, and unanimously cried out that they had most wickedly seduced them out of the light, they at length, to prevent a huge misfortune, confessed the same with sadness, and yet withal alleged that what had happened here was not to be animadverted upon them in the worst sense. For inasmuch as the lords were absolutely resolved to get into the castle, and had promised great sums of money to that effect, each one had used all craft to seize upon something, and so things were brought to that state that was now manifest before their eyes. But just because it had not succeeded, in their opinion, they had deserved no less than the lords themselves, who should have had so much understanding as to consider that, if anyone could be sure of getting in, he should not have clambered over the wall with them, that there should be so great peril for the sake of a slight gain.

Their books also sold so well, that whoever had no other means to maintain himself, had to engage in such a deception. They hoped moreover, that if a right judgment were made, they should be found in no way to have miscarried, for they had behaved themselves towards the lords, as became servants, upon their earnest entreaty.

But answer was made to them that his royal majesty had determined to punish them all, every man, although one more severely than another. For although what had been alleged by them was partly true, and therefore the lords should not wholly be indulged, yet they had good reason to prepare themselves for death, they who had so presumptuously obtruded themselves, and perhaps seduced the more ignorant against their will; as likewise those who had violated royal majesty with false books, for the same might be shown from their very writings and books.

Hereupon many began to lament, cry, weep, entreat and prostrate themselves most piteously, all of which notwithstanding could avail them nothing, and I marvelled much how the virgin could be so resolute, when their misery caused our eyes to run over, and moved our compassion (although the most part of them had procured us much trouble and vexation). For she presently dispatched her page, who brought with him all the cuirassiers who had this day been appointed at the scales, who were each of them commanded to take his own to him, and in an orderly procession, so that each cuirassier should go with one of the prisoners, to conduct them into her great garden. At which time each one so exactly recognised his own man, that I marvelled at it. Leave was also likewise given to my companions of yesterday to go out into the garden unbound, and to be present at the execution of the sentence. Now as soon as every man had come forth, the virgin mounted up into her high throne, requesting us to sit down upon the steps, and to appear at the judgment; which we did not refuse, but left everything standing upon the table (except the goblet, which the virgin committed to the pages' keeping) and went forth in our robes, upon the throne, which moved by itself gently as if we passed through the air, till in this manner we came into the garden, where we all arose together.

This garden was not extraordinarily curious, but it pleased me that the trees were planted in such good order. Besides, there ran in it a most costly fountain, adorned with wonderful figures and inscriptions and strange characters (which, God willing, I shall mention in a future book). In this garden was raised a wooden scaffold, hung about with curiously painted figured coverlets. Now there were four galleries made one over another; the first was more glorious than any of the rest, and therefore covered with a white taffeta curtain, so that at that time we could not perceive who was behind it. The second was empty and uncovered. Again the last two were covered with red and blue taffeta. Now as soon as we had come to the scaffold, the virgin bowed herself down to the ground, at which we were mightily terrified, for we could easily guess that the king and queen must not be far off. Now we also having duly performed our reverence, the virgin led us up by the winding stairs into the second gallery, where she placed herself uppermost, and us in our former order. But how the emperor whom I had released behaved himself towards me, both at this time and also before at the table, I cannot well relate without slander of wicked tongues. For he might well have imagined in what anguish and solicitude he should now have been, in case he were at present to attend the judgment with such ignominy, and that only through me he had now attained such dignity and worthiness.

Meanwhile the virgin who first of all brought me the invitation, and whom until now I had never since seen, came in. First she gave one blast upon her trumpet, and then with a very loud voice declared the sentence in this manner:

The King's Majesty, my most gracious Lord, could wish with all his heart that each and every one here assembled had upon his Majesty's invitation presented themselves so qualified as that they might (to his honour) with greatest frequency have adorned this his appointed nuptial and joyful feast. But since it has otherwise pleased Almighty God, his Majesty has nothing about which to murmur, but must be forced, contrary to his own inclination, to abide by the ancient and laudable constitutions of this kingdom. But now, so that his Majesty's innate clemency may be celebrated all over the world, he has so far absolutely dealt with his council and estates, that the usual sentence shall be considerably mitigated.

So in the first place he is willing to vouchsafe to the lords and potentates, not only their lives entirely, but also that he will freely and frankly dismiss them; kindly and courteously entreating your lordships not at all to take it in evil part that you cannot be present at his Majesty's feast of honour; but to remember that not more than you can duly and easily sustain is imposed upon your lordships by God Almighty (who in the distribution of his gifts has an incomprehensible consideration). Neither is your reputation hereby prejudiced, although you be rejected by this our order, since we cannot all of us do all things at once. But for as much as your lordships have been seduced by base rascals, it shall not, on their part, pass unrevenged.

And furthermore his Majesty resolves shortly to communicate to your Lordships a catalogue of heretics or *Index Expurgatorius,* that you may henceforth be able to discern between the good and the evil with better judgment. And because his Majesty before long also intends to rummage his library, and offer up the seductive writings to Vulcan, he kindly, humbly, and courteously entreats every one of your lordships to do the same with your own, whereby it is to be hoped that all evil and mischief may for the time to come be remedied. And you are withal to be admonished, never henceforth to covet an entrance here so inconsiderately, lest the former excuse about seducers be taken from you, and you fall into disgrace and contempt with all men.

Finally, for as much as the estates of the land still have something to demand of your lordships, his Majesty hopes that no man will think much to redeem himself with a chain or whatever else he has about him, and so in friendly manner to depart from us, and through our safe conduct to take himself home again.

The others who did not stand up to the first, third and fourth weight, his

Majesty will not so lightly dismiss. But so that they also may now experience his Majesty's compassion, it is his command to strip them stark naked and so send them forth. Those who in the second and fifth weight were found too light, shall besides stripping, be noted with one, two or more brand-marks, according as each one was lighter or heavier. They who were drawn up by the sixth or seventh, and not by the rest, shall be somewhat more graciously dealt with, and so forward. (For to every combination there was a certain punishment ordained, which is here too long to recount.) They who yesterday separated themselves freely of their own accord, shall go out at liberty without any blame.

Finally, the convicted vagabond-cheaters who could move up none of the weights, shall as occasion serves be punished in body and life, with the sword, halter, water and rods. And such execution of judgment shall be inviolably observed as an example to others.

Herewith our virgin broke her wand, and the other who read the sentence blew her trumpet, and stepped with most profound reverence towards those who stood behind the curtain.

But here I cannot omit to reveal something to the reader concerning the number of our prisoners, of whom those who weighed one, were seven; those who weighed two, were twenty one; they who three, thirty five; they who four, thirty five; those who five, twenty one; those who six, seven; but he that came to the seventh, and yet could not well raise it, he was only one, and indeed the same whom I released. Besides these, of them who wholly failed there were many; but of those who drew all the weights from the ground, but few. And as these each stood before us, so I diligently numbered them and noted them down in my table-book; and it is very admirable that amongst all those who weighed anything, none was equal to another. For although amongst those who weighed three, there were thirty five, yet one of them weighed the first, second, and third, another the third, fourth, and fifth, a third, the fifth, sixth, and seventh, and so on. It is likewise very wonderful that amongst one hundred and twenty six who weighed anything, none was equal to another; and I would very willingly name them all, with each man's weight, were it not as yet forbidden me. But I hope it may hereafter be published with the interpretation.

Now this judgment being read over, the lords in the first place were well satisfied, because in such severity they did not dare look for a mild sentence. So they gave more than was desired of them, and each one redeemed himself with chains, jewels, gold, money and other things, as much as they had about them, and with reverence took leave. Now although the king's servants were forbidden to jeer at any at his going away, yet some unlucky birds could not hold their laughter, and certainly it was sufficiently ridiculous to see them pack away with such speed, without once looking behind them. Some desired that the promised catalogue might at once be dispatched after them, and then they would take such order with their books as should be pleasing to his majesty; which was again assured. At the door was given to each of them out of a cup a Draught of Forgetfulness, so that he might have no further memory of misfortune.

After these the volunteers departed, who because of their ingenuity were allowed to pass, but yet so as never to return again in the same fashion. But if to them (as likewise to the others) anything further were revealed, then they should be welcome guests.

Meanwhile others were stripping, in which also an inequality (according to each man's demerit) was observed. Some were sent away naked, without other hurt. Others were driven out with small bells. Some were scourged forth. In brief the punishments were so various, that I am not able to recount them all. In the end it came to the last, with whom a somewhat longer time was spent, for while some were being hung, some beheaded, some forced to leap into the water, and the rest otherwise being dispatched, much time was consumed. Truly at this execution my eyes ran over, not indeed in regard of the punishment, which they for their impudency well deserved, but in contemplation of human blindness, in that we are continually busying ourselves in that which ever since the first Fall has been hitherto sealed up to us. Thus the garden which so recently was quite full, was soon emptied, so that besides the soldiers there was not a man left.

Now as soon as this was done, and silence had been kept for the space of five minutes, there came forth a beautiful snow-white unicorn with a golden collar (having on it certain letters) about his neck. In the same place he bowed himself down upon both his forefeet, as if hereby he had shown honour to the lion, who stood so immovably upon the fountain, that I had taken him to be of stone or brass. The lion immediately took the naked sword which he had in his paw, and broke it in two in the middle, and the pieces of it, it seemed to me, sunk into the fountain; after which he roared for so long, until a white dove brought a branch of olive in her bill, which the lion devoured in an instant, and so was quieted. And so the unicorn returned to his place with joy.

Hereupon our virgin led us down again by the winding stairs from the scaffold, and so we again made our reverence towards the curtain. We were to wash our hands and heads in the fountain, and there to wait a little while in our order, till the king was again returned into his hall through a certain secret gallery, and then we were also conducted into our former lodging with choice music, pomp, state, and pleasant discourse. And this was done about four in the afternoon. But so that in the meantime the time might not seem too long to us, the virgin bestowed on each of us a noble page, who were not only richly dressed, but also exceedingly learned, so that they could so aptly discourse upon all subjects that we had good reason to be ashamed of ourselves. These were commanded to lead us up and down the castle, but only into certain places, and if possible, to shorten the time according to our desire. Meanwhile the virgin took leave with this consolation, that at supper she would be with us again, and after that celebrate the ceremonies of the hanging up of the weights, requesting that we would in patience wait till the next day, for on the morrow we must be presented to the king.

She having thus departed from us, each of us did what best pleased him. One part viewed the excellent paintings, which they copied out for themselves, and considered also what the wonderful characters might signify. Others wanted to occupy themselves again with meat and drink.

I caused my page to conduct me (together with my companion) up and down the castle, which walk I shall never regret as long as I have a day to live. For besides many other glorious antiquities, the royal sepulchre was also showed to me, by which I learned more than is extant in all books. There in the same place stands also the glorious phoenix (about which, two years ago, I published a particular small discourse).

And I am resolved (in case this narration shall prove useful) to set forth several particular treatises concerning the lion, eagle, griffin, falcon and the like, together with their draughts and inscriptions. It grieves me for my other companions, that they neglected such precious treasures. And yet I cannot but think it was the special will of God that it should be so. I indeed reaped the most benefit from my page, for according as each one's genius lay, so he led whoever was entrusted to him into the quarters and places which were pleasing to him.

Now the keys belonging hereunto were committed to my page, and therefore this good fortune happened to me before the rest; for although he invited others to come in, yet they imagining such tombs to be only in the churchyard, thought they should get there well enough, whenever anything was to be seen there. Neither shall these monuments (as both of us copied and transcribed them) be withheld from my thankful scholars. The other thing that was shown to us two was the noble library as it was all together before the Reformation. Of which (although it makes my heart rejoice as often as I call it to mind) I have so much the less to say, because the catalogue of it is very shortly to be published. At the entry to this room stands a great book, the like of which I never saw, in which all the figures, rooms, portals, also all the writings, riddles and the like, to be seen in the whole castle, are delineated. Now although we made a promise concerning this also, yet at present I must contain myself, and first learn to know the world better. In every book stands its author painted; of which (as I understood) many were to be burnt, so that even their memory might be blotted out from amongst the righteous.

Now having taken a full view of this, and having scarcely gone forth, another page came running to us, and having whispered something in our page's ear, he delivered up the keys to him, who immediately carried them up the winding stairs. But our page was very much out of countenance, and we having set hard upon him with entreaties, he declared to us that the king's majesty would by no means permit that either of the two, namely the library and sepulchres, should be seen by any man, and therefore he besought us as we cared for his life, to reveal this to no man, he having already utterly denied it. Whereupon both of us stood hovering between joy and fear, yet it continued in silence, and no man made further enquiry about it. Thus in both places we passed three hours, which I do not at all repent.

Now although it had already struck seven, yet nothing had so far been given us to eat; however, our hunger was easy to abate by constant revivings, and I could be well content to fast all my life long with such entertainment. About this time the curious fountains, mines, and all kinds of art-shops, were also shown to us, of which there was none but surpassed all our arts, even if they should all be melted into one mass. All their chambers were built in a semi-circle, so that they might have before their eyes the costly clockwork which was erected upon a fair turret in the centre, and regulate themselves according to the course of the planets, which were to be seen on it in a glorious manner. And hence I could easily conjecture where our artists failed; however it's none of my duty to inform them.

At length I came into a spacious room (shown indeed to the rest a great while before) in the middle of which stood a terrestrial globe, whose diameter was thirty feet, although nearly half of it, except a little which was covered with the steps, was let into the earth. Two men might readily turn this globe about with all its furniture, so that no more of it was ever to be seen, just so much as was above the horizon. Now although I could easily conceive that this was of some special use, yet I could not understand what those ringlets of gold (which were upon it in several places) served for; at which my page laughed, and advised me to view them more closely. In brief, I found there my native country noted in gold also; whereupon my companion sought his, and found that so too. Now for as much as the same happened in a similar way to the rest who stood by, the page told us for certain that it was yesterday declared to the king's majesty by their old Atlas (so is the astronomer named) that all the gilded points exactly answered to their native countries, according as had been shown to each of them. And therefore he also, as soon as he perceived that I undervalued myself and that nevertheless there stood a point upon my native country, moved one of the captains to entreat for us that we should be set upon the scale (without peril) at all adventures; especially seeing one of our native countries had a notable good mark. And truly it was not without reason that he, the page who had the greatest power of all the rest, was bestowed on me. For this I then returned him thanks, and immediately looked more diligently upon my native country, and found moreover that besides the ringlet, there were also certain delicate streaks upon it, which nevertheless I would not be thought to speak about to my own praise and glory.

I saw much more too upon this globe than I am willing to reveal. Let each man take into consideration why every city does not produce a philosopher. After this he led us right into the globe, which was thus made: on the sea (there being a large square beside it) was a tablet, on which stood three dedications and the author's name, which a man might gently lift up and by a little joined board go into the centre, which was capable of holding four persons, being nothing but a round board on which we could sit, and at ease, by broad daylight (it was now already dark) contemplate the stars. To my thinking they were mere carbuncles which glittered in an agreeable order, and moved so gallantly that I had scarcely any mind ever to go out again, as the page afterwards told the virgin, with which she often teased me.

For it was already supper-time, and I had so much amused myself in the globe, that I was almost the last at the table; so I made no more delay, but having put on my gown again (which I had before laid aside) and stepping to the table, the waiters treated me with so much reverence and honour, that for shame I dared not look up, and so unawares permitted the virgin, who attended me on one side, to stand, which she soon perceiving, twitched me by the gown, and so led me to the table. To speak any further concerning the music, or the rest of that magnificent entertainment, I hold it needless, both because it is not possible to express it well enough, and because I have reported it above according to my power. In brief, there was nothing there but art and amenity.

Now after we had related our employment since noon to each other (however, not a word was spoken of the library and monuments), being already merry with the wine, the virgin began thus: "My Lords, I have a great contention with one of my sisters. In our chamber we have an eagle. Now we cherish him with such diligence, that each of us is desirous to be the best beloved, and upon that score we have many a squabble. One day we concluded to go both together to him, and toward whom he should show himself most friendly, hers should he properly be. This we need, and I (as commonly) carried in my hand a branch of laurel, but my sister had none. Now as soon as he saw us both, he immediately gave my sister another branch which he had in his beak, and reached for mine, which I gave him. Now each of us hereupon imagined herself to be best beloved of him; which way am I to resolve myself?"

This modest proposal of the virgin pleased us all mighty well, and each one would gladly have heard the solution, but inasmuch as they all looked to me, and wanted me to begin, my mind was so extremely confounded that I knew not what else to do with it but propound another in its stead, and therefore said: "Gracious Lady, your Ladyship's question would easily be resolved if one thing did not perplex me. I had two companions, both of which loved me exceedingly; now they being doubtful which of them was most dear to me, concluded to run to me, I unawares, and that he whom I should then embrace should be the right. This they did, yet one of them could not keep pace with the other, so he stayed behind and wept, the other I embraced with amazement. Now when they had afterwards discovered the business to me, I did not know how to resolve myself, and have since then let it rest in this manner, until I may find some good advice herein."

The virgin wondered at it, and well observed whereabout I was, whereupon she replied, "Well then, let us both be quit," and then desired the solution from the rest.

But I had already made them wise. So the next began thus. "In the city where I live, a virgin was recently condemned to death, but the judge, being somewhat pitiful towards her, caused it to be proclaimed that if any man desired to become the virgin's champion, he should have free leave to do it. Now she had two lovers; the one presently made himself ready, and came into the lists to await his adversary; afterwards the other also presented himself, but coming somewhat too late, he resolved nevertheless to fight, and willingly suffer himself to be vanquished, so that the virgin's life might be preserved, which also succeeded accordingly. Whereupon each challenged her. Now my Lords, instruct me, to which of them of right does she belong?"

The virgin could hold out no longer, but said, "I thought to have gained much information, and have got myself into the net, but yet would gladly hear whether there are any more to come."

"Yes, that there are," answered the third, "a stranger adventure has not yet been recounted than that which happened to me. In my youth I loved a worthy maid: now so that my love might attain its desired end, I used to employ an ancient matron, who easily brought me to her. Now it happened that the maid's brethren came in upon us just as we three were together, and were in such a rage that they would have taken my life, but upon my vehement supplication, they at length forced me to swear to take each of them for a year, to be my wedded wife. Now tell me, my Lords, should I take the old, or the young one first?"

We all laughed sufficiently at this riddle, and though some of them muttered to one another about it, yet would none undertake to unfold it.

Hereupon the fourth began: "In a certain city there dwelt an honourable lady, who was beloved of all, but especially by a young nobleman, who was too importunate with her. At length she gave him this determination, that if he could lead her into a fair green garden of roses in a cold winter, then he should obtain what he desired, but if not, he must resolve never to see her again. The nobleman travelled to all countries to find such a man as might perform this, till at length he found a little old man that promised to do it for him, if he would assure him of half his estate; which he having consented to the other, was as good as his word. Whereupon he invited the aforesaid lady to his garden, where, contrary to her expectation, she found all things green, pleasant and warm, and remembering her promise, she only requested that she might once more return to her husband, to whom with sighs and tears she bewailed her lamentable condition. But because he sufficiently perceived her faithfulness, he dispatched her back to her lover who had so dearly purchased her, so that she might give him satisfaction. This husband's integrity did so mightily affect the nobleman, that he thought it a sin to touch so honest a wife; so he sent her home again with honour to her lord. Now the little man perceiving such faith in both these, would not, however poor he was, be the least in honour, but restored to the nobleman all his goods again and went his way. Now, my lords, I know not which of these persons may have shown the greatest faithfulness and honour?"

Here our tongues were quite cut off. Neither would the virgin make any other reply, but only that another should go on.

So the fifth, without delay, began: "My Lords, I do not wish to make long work of this; who has the greater joy, he that beholds what he loves, or he that only thinks on it?"

"He that beholds it," said the virgin.

"No," I answered.

Hereupon a debate arose, so the sixth called out, "My lords, I am to take a wife; now I have before me a maid, a married wife, and a widow; ease me of this doubt, and I will afterwards help to order the rest."

"It goes well there," replied the seventh, "where a man has a choice, but with me the case is otherwise. In my youth I loved a fair and virtuous virgin from the bottom of my heart, and she loved me in similar manner; however, because of her friends' denial we could not come together in wedlock. Whereupon she was married to another, yet an honest and discreet person, who maintained her honourably and with affection, until she came to the pains of childbirth, which went so hard for her that all thought she was dead, so with much state and great mourning she was interred. Now I thought to myself, during her life you could have no part in this woman, but now she is dead you may embrace and kiss her sufficiently; so I took my servant with me, who dug her up by night. Now having opened the coffin and locked her in my arms, feeling about her heart, I found some little motion in it still, which increased more and more from my warmth, till at last I perceived that she was indeed still alive. So I quietly bore her home, and after I had warmed her chilled body with a costly bath of herbs, I committed her to my mother until she brought forth a fair son, whom I caused to be nursed faithfully, as for his mother. After two days (she being then in great amazement) I revealed to her all the preceding affair, requesting her for the time to come to live with me as a wife; against this she found exception, in case it should be grievous to her husband who had maintained her well and honourably. But if it could be otherwise, she was obliged at present to love one as well as the other. Now after two months (being then about to make a journey elsewhere) I invited her husband as a guest, and amongst other things asked him whether, if his deceased wife should come home again, he would be content to receive her. He affirmed it with tears and lamentations, and I brought him his wife together with his son, and gave an account of all the preceding business, entreating him to ratify with his consent my intended espousals. After a long dispute he could not deny me my right, but had to leave me his wife. But there was still a debate about the son."

Here the virgin interrupted him, and said, "It makes me wonder how you could double the afflicted man's grief."

"What," he answered, "Was it not my right?" Upon this there arose a dispute amongst us, yet most affirmed that he had done right. "No," he said, "I freely returned him both his wife and his son. Now tell me, my Lords, was my honesty, or this man's joy, the greater?"

These words had so much cheered the virgin that (as if it had been for the sake of these two) she caused a health to be drunk.

After which the rest of the proposals went on somewhat perplexedly, so that I could not retain them all; yet this comes to my mind, that one said that a few years before he had seen a physician, who brought a parcel of wood against winter, with which he warmed himself all winter long; but as soon as the spring returned he sold the very same wood again, and so had use of it for nothing.

"Here there must be skill," said the virgin, "but the time is now past."

"Yes," replied my companion, "whoever does not understand how to resolve all the riddles may give each man notice of it by a proper messenger, and he will not be denied."

At this time they began to say grace, and we arose all together from the table, satisfied and merry rather than satiated; and it is to be wished that all invitations and feastings were kept like this. Having now taken a few turns up and down the hall again, the virgin asked us whether we desired to begin the wedding.

"Yes, noble and virtuous lady," said one. Whereupon she privately despatched a page, and yet in the meantime proceeded in discourse with us. In brief she had already become so familiar with us, that I ventured to request her name. The virgin smiled at my curiosity, but yet was not moved, but replied: "My name contains five and fifty, and yet has only eight letters; the third is the third part of the fifth, which added to the sixth will produce a number whose root shall exceed the third itself by just the first, and it is the half of the fourth. Now the fifth and the seventh are equal, the last and the fifth are also equal, and make with the second as much as the sixth, which contains just four more than the third tripled. Now tell me, my lord, what am I called?"

The answer was intricate enough to me, yet I did not leave off, but said, "Noble and virtuous lady, may I not have only one letter?"

"Yes," she said, "that may well be done."

"What then," I replied again, "may the seventh contain?"

"It contains," she said, "as many as there are lords here."

With this I was content, and easily found her name, at which she was very pleased, and assured us that much more should yet be revealed to us.

Meantime certain virgins had made themselves ready, and came in with great ceremony. First of all two youths carried lights before them; one of them was of jocund countenance, sprightly eyes and gentle proportion. The other looked rather angry, and whatever he would have, must be, as I afterwards perceived. After them first followed four virgins. One looked shame-facedly towards the earth, very humble in behaviour. The second also was a modest, bashful virgin. The third, as she entered the room, seemed amazed at something, and as I understood, she cannot easily abide where there is too much mirth. The fourth brought with her certain small wreaths, thereby to manifest her kindness and liberality.

After these four came two who were somewhat more gloriously apparelled; they saluted us courteously. One of them had a gown of sky colour spangled with golden stars. The other's was green, beautified with red and white stripes. On their heads they had thin flying kerchiefs, which adorned them most becomingly.

At last came one on her own, who had a coronet on her head, but looked up towards heaven rather than towards earth. We all thought it was the Bride, but were much mistaken, although otherwise in honour, riches and state she much surpassed the Bride; and she afterwards ruled the whole wedding. Now on this occasion we all followed our virgin, and fell down on our knees; however, she showed herself to be extremely humble, offering everyone her hand, and admonishing us not to be too much surprised at this, for this was one of her smallest bounties; but to lift up our eyes to our Creator, and learn hereby to acknowledge his omnipotency, and so proceed in our enterprise, employing this grace to the praise of God, and the good of man. In sum, her words were quite different from those of our virgin, who was somewhat more worldly. They pierced me through even to my bones and marrow.

"And you," she said further to me, "have received more than others, see that you also make a larger return." This to me was a very strange sermon; for as soon as we saw the virgins with the music, we imagined we must soon begin to dance, but that time was not as yet come. Now the weights, which have been mentioned before, stood still in the same place, so the duchess (I knew not yet who she was) commanded each virgin to take up one, but to our virgin she gave her own, which was the last and greatest, and commanded us to follow behind. Our majesty was then somewhat abated, for I observed well that our virgin was too good for us, and we were not so highly reputed as we ourselves were almost in part willing to fantasise. So we went behind in our order, and were brought into the first chamber, where our virgin in the first place hung up the duchess' weight, during which an excellent spiritual hymn was sung. There was nothing costly in this room save only curious little prayer books which should never be missing. In the middle was erected a pulpit, very convenient for prayer, in which the duchess kneeled down, and about her we all had to kneel and pray after the virgin, who read out of a book, that this wedding might tend to the honour of God, and our own benefit. Afterwards we came into the second chamber, where the first virgin hung up her weight too, and so forward until all the ceremonies were finished. Hereupon the duchess again presented her hand to everyone, and departed hence with her virgin.

Our president stayed yet a while with us. But because it had already been night for two hours, she would no longer detain us. I thought she was glad of our company, yet she bade us good night, and wished us quiet rest, and so departed in a friendly manner, although unwillingly, from us. Our pages were well instructed in their business, and therefore showed every man his chamber, and stayed with us too in another bed, so that in case we wanted anything we might make use of them. My chamber (of the rest I am not able to speak) was royally furnished with rare tapestries, and hung about with paintings. But above all things I delighted in my page, who was so excellently spoken, and experienced in the arts, that he spent yet another hour with me, and it was half past three when I first fell asleep. And this was the first night that I slept in quiet, and yet a scurvy dream would not let me rest; for all the night I was troubled with a door which I could not get open, but at last I did it. With these fantasies I passed the time, till at length towards day I awakened.

The Third Day: Commentary

The events that are enacted on the third day have little or no relationship to earthly values and principles. Everything that has value as measured by earthly standards suddenly turns out to have less or even no value at all in this world. And conversely, what was insignificant in earthly human relationships – here it suddenly "carries weight." How can we form a picture of this measuring by other standards in the spiritual world? We can have a glimpse of it when a dying person, who gradually looks at his or her own life with different eyes, reevaluates it, and may then suddenly say: "Everything is becoming so different." This is what someone actually said shortly before dying.

The classic example of this transition is an anecdote from the Middle Ages. Two monks have an agreement: the first to die will try to appear to the surviving one in a dream or as a spiritual apparition to tell him what things look like over there. They agree on two passwords: things are either *taliter* (the same) or *aliter* (different). After one of them has died he stands at night at the foot of his brother's bed and says loudly: *Totaliter aliter!* Totally different!

The other example, a dream, demonstrates how differently things are judged in the world of the spirit, which is also the world of the deceased. August Pauli, a priest in the pioneering days of The Christian Community, had a friend who had an important position in society, and who was used to being met with respect in daily life: literally and figuratively a "weighty" person. When this man died, he appeared after some time in a dream to August Pauli. In the image of the dream he had lost all his "weight" and "weightiness"; he stood there as a skinny little man and said with a guilty look: "Yes, this is all that is left of me."

Everything becomes very different, also on the third day of the *Chymical Wedding*, which brings irrevocable decisions and partings. When on this day the virgin (only later will we hear who she is) enters the hall, she is pleased that a group of the guests have "submitted [themselves] to the yoke." Christian Rosenkreutz and his companions voluntarily took on a burden. Those who remained in the hall had to spend the night powerless and motionless. The others afforded themselves certain privileges by spending the night in rooms of their own. Apparently Christian Rosenkreutz has already become special to the virgin, for she addresses him in particular.

The path he follows has to do with what in the tradition of initiation practices is called the "golden rule." To be sure, there are ways of spiritual development today that hold out the prospect of a straight assault on seventh heaven – but there are also some methods that lead to the goal only very slowly and gradually. These latter methods follow the golden rule: "For every single step that you take in seeking knowledge of hidden truths, you must take three steps in perfecting your character toward the good."[1] Apparently that is what Christian Rosenkreutz is doing. From the outside it looks as if he is not getting very far. He follows the slow road.

The virgin is surrounded by two hundred armed men who soon receive their own task for each of the condemned men. The previous evening she had been surrounded by little lights that followed her, and Christian Rosenkreutz had wondered whether these lights were her servants. In whatever form they appear – as lights or as the ones who execute the sentence – they are spiritual powers that act by order of a higher being. Christian tradition is familiar with angels as messengers of higher hierarchies. Such a spiritual being is connected with every human being on earth. Not only does the higher world judge the life of each separate human being but, whether they want to or not, human beings take their angels with them on their path. In this regard, St Paul wrote the remarkable words: "You also know that even the destiny of the angels is decided through us" (1Cor.6:3 *M*). When human beings have to go through troubles on earth or in life after death, their angels have to follow them. The armed men, who are later entrusted to each of the condemned ones, have in a certain sense a similar task.

We have to picture the virgin as an extremely mobile person; she jumps down from her high throne, wanders about among the guests, divides them into seven groups after the seven weights have been put in place, and then jumps back onto her throne. It may not be easy to picture such a prominent person moving about in that way, but it shows something of the fluidity of her character.

Richard Kienast relates the seven weights to the seven virtues that were practised from the early days of Christianity (which go back to Aurelius Clemens Prudentius, 348–410):

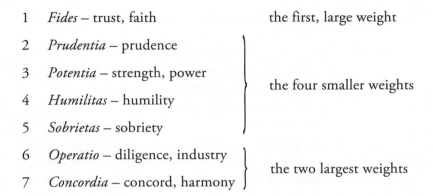

1 *Fides* – trust, faith — the first, large weight

2 *Prudentia* – prudence

3 *Potentia* – strength, power

4 *Humilitas* – humility — the four smaller weights

5 *Sobrietas* – sobriety

6 *Operatio* – diligence, industry

7 *Concordia* – concord, harmony — the two largest weights

In the Middle Ages, and still at the time of Valentin Andreae, people were familiar with the motif of the conflict between the seven virtues and the seven vices.

In his essay on the *Chymical Wedding*, Rudolf Steiner creates a relationship between the seven weights and the seven liberal arts:

1 *Grammatica*

2 *Dialectica*

3 *Rhetorica*

4 *Musica*

5 *Arithmetica*

6 *Geometria*

7 *Astronomia*

These two different approaches certainly should not exclude each other. In its time the practice of the seven liberal arts also included the practice of the seven virtues, moral qualities. The practice of arithmetica, for instance, fostered a certain quality of sobriety. A person who thoroughly occupied himself with the old form of astronomy brought about inner harmony, concordia. In the seventeenth century the astronomer Kepler spoke of the "harmony of the spheres." In former times, the practice of the sciences still had a moral character: the practice of the seven virtues.

At the decisive moment of the weighing all outer pretence evaporates:

> And who will to a wedding come
> And has not bidden been,
> And yet doth come with much display
> Will yet be mocked by everyone.

Arranged by social position – first the emperors, then kings, lords, nobility, scholars, and finally charlatans and quacks – the guests are weighed. The first of the emperors, who tips the scale only with the last weight, evokes Christian Rosenkreutz's compassion. He proves to be too light for the last weight, the spiritual harmony among the virtues *(concordia)*, while he had passed the six preceding virtues. One has to have a certain moral weight to keep one's footing in this new world.

Then there are those who enter into the spiritual world with "borrowed wisdom." Such people don't make the grade. That is what happens to the second emperor, who carries a great thick book under his robe, until he drops it, to the great amusement of the spectators. More often than not the judgment turns out different from what Christian Rosenkreutz had expected. This world is *totaliter aliter!* He says: "I cannot leave unmentioned that few of those great personages held out. However, various eminent virtues (beyond my hopes) were found in many." Here he literally uses the word "virtues" in connection with the weighing.

All the guests, without exception, are weighed. What they show on the outside has no weight. What you are, is all that counts.

When at last everyone is weighed and many are found too light, one of the captains says: "Gracious Madam, if it please your Ladyship, let these poor men who acknowledged their misunderstanding be set upon the scale too, without their incurring any danger of penalty, and only for recreation's sake, if perhaps anything that is right may be found amongst them."

So they too, trembling with fear, are weighed. Christian Rosenkreutz is the eighth of them. And then the unexpected happens:

> Now as soon as (with trembling) I stepped up, my companion
> who already sat by in his velvet looked kindly upon me, and

the virgin herself smiled a little. But for as much as I outstood all the weights, the virgin commanded them to draw me up by force, wherefore three men also hung on the other side of the beam, and yet nothing could prevail. Whereupon one of the pages immediately stood up, and cried out exceedingly loud, *"That is he."*

Upon which the other replied, "Then let him gain his liberty," which the virgin accorded.

Christian Rosenkreutz arrived at the eleventh hour, maybe even as the last person. When he is weighed he is next to last, the eighth in line. That is what Goethe calls in his scene of the Cabiri in *Faust:* "The eighth whom no one had noticed." This last one, who deems himself unworthy, suddenly turns out to be the first. From this moment, he moves through the spiritual world on a path that is all his own, in freedom. While henceforth the others go their way as a group, he takes his own way, literally and figuratively. From now on he has a surplus; he works with forces that have been freed. Out of this he is able, as a free deed, to liberate the first emperor, who had just lacked something – thus transforming his compassion into a deed. We are ourselves familiar with such surplus forces: love. Significantly, Rudolf Steiner writes in his essay: "For of all the soul forces already developed in the sense world, love is the only one that can remain unchanged by the passage of the soul into the spiritual world."[2]

At the request of the virgin, he gives her the four roses he had on his hat. In many other situations, from being a receiver he now becomes a giver.

The sentences that are now proclaimed differ for each of the prisoners. Only "those who the day before willingly surrendered themselves, might be allowed to depart without any blame" – even though they have been found too light in the weighing. Just as everyone has his own individual weight, they also receive their own individual judgment.

Now there is a new order. People are arranged at table according to their ranking, but this ranking looks quite different from the former one. Those who made it through the weighing have acquired a new capacity: they can see the servants, who are invisible to the others.

As confirmation of this phase of the initiation they are all presented with the golden fleece with a flying lion. Both symbols are well-known in alchemy, and from even earlier times. For instance, a Greek myth tells of Jason who on the voyage of the Argonauts captured the golden fleece, the golden hide of a ram. It was the search for the original powers of the soul life, which had not yet been clouded by desire and egotism. The alchemists knew the symbol of "winged gold" – *aurum volatile* – also indicating the unclouded soul forces, the pure power of the heart.

When everyone has been assigned his place at table, Christian Rosenkreutz subtly observes that he receives a special place – where exactly he prefers not to say. It is the greatest of all arts for the most developed human being to remain the most modest one and take no advantage of his position. It reminds me of a particular degree of spiritual development that the Russian saints called the Order of the Starets. One of the most famous among them was the Russian St Seraphim of Sarov (1754–1833). He bowed to the ground for everyone who entered his hermit's cell, be it a criminal, vagabond, burgher or monk, and he invariably greeted them with the words: "My joy!" This is the stage of development at which Christian Rosenkreutz has arrived: when grandness becomes little, and the human being bows down.

The virgin gives the decorated ones a drink from the chalice of Fortuna, the goddess of fortune, which makes Christian Rosenkreutz sad, because he is "all too well acquainted with fortune's waywardness." Later in the day the prisoners receive something else to drink, namely the Draught of Forgetfulness. Those who have to leave this realm in order to return to earthly reality must forget everything they have experienced here. In ancient Greece it was still known that "truth" came from a memory of the spiritual world before birth. The Greek word for truth is *aletheia,* literally "not through Lethe," the river that separated the realm of the living from that of the unborn and deceased. On its way to birth, the soul had to wade through Lethe, so that on earth it would forget its origin; and similarly, in reverse, the soul of the deceased on its way to the underworld. But whenever, as a human being on earth, one discovered an element of truth, it was said that one remembered something that had not passed through the river Lethe: *a-letheia.* Here, however, everything the wrongful guests have experienced must be completely forgotten.

The proclamation with the judgments that is read by the virgin consists of two parts. Accordingly, the prisoners are divided into two groups, one group consisting of the gullible ones who unthinkingly accepted what the books of false alchemists concocted for them. They overestimated themselves and did not sufficiently practise self-knowledge. The second group committed a serious crime; these are the ones who wrote these books and knowingly deceived people. They have to prepare themselves for capital punishment. Even in our legal world of today we still distinguish between these two forms of crime. When someone through circumstances finds himself in a hard corner and commits a crime, he is judged differently from the one who commits a premeditated crime. In this way we might picture the difference between the two groups.

Each of the prisoners is accompanied by his own armed warrior, his hierarchical being that judges him with his own individual penalty. "Each one so exactly recognised his own man, that I marvelled at it," says Christian Rosenkreutz. They are inseparably linked to each other.

The garden where the sentences are executed is a strange one. "This garden was not extraordinarily curious, but it pleased me that the trees were planted in such good order." At this stage we are certainly not yet in Paradise! In the garden stands a wooden structure with four levels – a classic indication of four heavens, four worlds above humanity. Apparently, behind a curtain concealing the first level the king and queen are hidden; the virgin makes a reverent bow.

In reading the final judgment, against all pronouncements made to this point, the virgin still bestows mercy on a large group of the prisoners. The sentence is mitigated. But the books of the false alchemists will be burned. Valentin Andreae also used this picture in his *Confessio*. He knew all too well that the royal art of alchemy was not only cultivated but also misused. Here he fulminated against the books of the false alchemists, "in so much as they spared not even the divine Trinity, but accustomed themselves to cheat people all the country over." We are familiar with the stories about alchemists who promised mountains of gold and purloined a few pieces of gold from their gullible followers. The *Fama* calls the making of gold a trifling work of the art of alchemy, a sideline.

It is true that on earth false alchemy has taken root, but in *this* world it cannot exist. That is an important element in the judgment. In the world where Christian Rosenkreutz now finds himself, a part of human life has no say; it has to be radically banished. In part it must even be exterminated, purged.

The Italian painter Segantini (1858–99) relates something of this reality from a dream. He dreamed that a dark, repulsive being appeared to him. Twice he chased this being away.

> Then I said to myself: "Perhaps I should not have chased it away; it will want to revenge itself." Hardly had I spoken this thought when a man, who looked like a priest, took me by my arm and led me to an altar on which a golden tabernacle was standing. He opened it, and I saw the coffin of a little child which he closed again, upon which he struck the lid three times with a hammer. He then turned to me and said: "This is a piece of you."
>
> And I replied: "There was a soul in this child; a part of my soul. This dead child is part of my flesh. The soul is up there – for I sense that a part of me is near God."
>
> At that moment I burst into tears. In my dream I went into the next room, threw myself on a large bed and wept incessantly, until I woke up with tears on my face.

These are drastic pictures that remind us of the images of the Book of Revelation. There we find the imagery that says that a third part of humanity was killed. What third part? A third of the human being, the part that is called the spirit, is threatened with destruction in apocalyptic times. On earth body and soul have the right to exist, but the human spirit is killed.

Before the sentences are executed, the virgin breaks her staff in two. In antiquity the judge would do this when the accused was found guilty. It is the staff of the independent "I", the strength of which is in a certain sense broken. The accused is no longer able to follow his own will.

What then follows is a typical example of the symbolism of numbers that was practised in Andreae's time. Kienast interpreted this symbolism. For Andreae the point is to show that each of the 126 guests has a unique "soul weight."

Sometimes the details in the story of the *Chymical Wedding* help us understand a lot of things at the same time. When the prisoners are executed Christian Rosenkreutz says: "Truly at this execution my eyes ran over, not indeed in regard of the punishment, which they for their impudency well deserved, but in contemplation of human blindness, in that we are continually busying ourselves in that which ever since the first Fall has been hitherto sealed up to us." He is very careful and precise in his use of the words "they" and "we." Although he need not submit to a judgment, he sympathises with the condemned men – knowing that every human being, including himself, is entangled in the consequences of the fall into sin. Every human being feels the urge to return to the lost paradise, but are we prepared for it?

When the sentences have been executed, there is a sudden pause in the press of events. Even this world momentarily holds its breath – and then appears a new imagination. The white unicorn is in alchemy the image of controlled, purified passion, just as the dark unicorn signifies uncontrolled forces of will. The unicorn kneels before the lion as if to pay tribute to it. Next, the lion breaks in two the sword that he was holding in his claws. "After which he roared for so long, until a white dove brought a branch of olive in her bill, which the lion devoured in an instant, and so was quieted. And so the unicorn returned to his place with joy." It is a foreshadowing of a future world in which violence has been overcome, a harbinger of the New Jerusalem described in the Book of Revelation. In his *Novella,* Goethe says of this future creation: "Lions shall become lambs."

Those who have survived the weighing disperse accompanied by their guides who take them on a tour of the castle. Christian Rosenkreutz again goes his own way, which takes him, as it turns out, to places he is not supposed to enter, namely the library and the tombs of the kings, where "I learned more than is extant in all books." The imagination of the phoenix appears here for the first time, the image of sacrifice that creates new life. He now comes to know this power.

More than by all the precious things and works of art, Christian Rosenkreutz is fascinated by a terrestrial globe, part of which is hidden in the ground. It is so large that he can climb into it through an opening and look through it to the outside. This takes us back to the alchemical motto in the picture shown with the events of the first day: "Visit the interior of the earth." This picture becomes even more significant when we consider that this is the third day, Holy Saturday, one of the days of which Christ announced before his Passion: "So will the Son of man be three days and three nights in the heart of the earth." (Mt.12:40) These words refer to Holy Saturday in particular.

Christian Rosenkreutz is so immersed in his observations of the earth that he forgets the time. In certain places the globe has small golden rings that catch his attention. His companion shows him that there is such a ring in the home countries of all the persons who have survived the weighing. When an angel or archangel looks at the earth it can be expected that he will observe something different from what astronauts or miners see. The hierarchies see that the earth shines in some places. Wherever initiates live, the earth radiates. An old German expression calls an initiate Meister Güldenfuss – Master Goldenfoot – because it was known that, wherever he goes, the initiate leaves footprints of "gold," spiritual golden rays. Christian Rosenkreutz also recognises a couple of golden stripes in his home country, but he prefers not to say anything more about them. He does not want to admit that, viewed from this world, he is ahead of the others.

When from the inside of the globe he sees the stars shining like garnets he really does not want to leave anymore, with the result that he is again the last to join the group.

A very strange conversation then develops at the dinner table. It can't really be called a conversation; rather it is a series of riddles that are strung together like a chain. The virgin asks a question, but she receives no answer. In its place follows another riddle. Whoever tries to arrive at answers to the questions that are being asked ends up losing all his spiritual substance. Only hair-splitting sophists can find reason in these questions. This is an eloquent example of the motto of the *Chymical Wedding*: "Secrets revealed lose their value." Rudolf Steiner wrote in his essay: "Among the company in which Christian Rosenkreutz finds himself, questions are propounded, all leading to the end that decisive answers are withheld. Reality is richer than the faculty of judgment based upon the intellect nurtured by the sense world."[3]

In the conversation that now follows – the virgin is becoming more and more intimate with the guests – Christian Rosenkreutz asks her name. In reply she gives him a riddle that leads him to the name Alchimia.

The figures who now enter the room express a range of moods: joy, humility, chastity, love. We again encounter a number of virtues guided by a crowned woman. "We all thought it was the Bride, but were much mistaken, although otherwise in honour, riches and state she much surpassed the Bride; and she afterwards ruled the whole wedding." From the words she speaks, many people infer that she is Theologia, although Wisdom, Sophia, is also mentioned.[4] Afterward she is called both duchess and queen. She is mentioned again on the seventh day when the king has received the petition of the guardian; she then rides beside the queen of the *Chymical Wedding*.

The seventh and last of the virtues mentioned above imposes a special task on Christian Rosenkreutz: "'And you,' she said further to me, 'have received more than others, see that you also make a larger return'."

She predicts that he will have to give up a great deal on his path.

Six of the seven new arrivals carry a weight; Theologia gives the last weight, the heaviest, *Concordia,* to the virgin to carry. Each of the seven weights are ultimately hung in a separate room, accompanied by prayers.

Again on this third day there is a dream: "All the night I was troubled with a door which I could not get open, but at last I did it." We will encounter this motif repeatedly in the coming days. But the dreams come to an end. Instead, a sleepless night following the fourth day will yield a secret.

The Fourth Day

The Fourth Day

I was still lying in my bed, and leisurely surveying all the noble images and figures up and down about my chamber, when suddenly I heard the music of cornets, as if they were already in procession. My page jumped out of the bed as if he had been at his wit's end, and looked more like one dead than living. In what state I was then is easily imaginable, for he said, "The rest are already presented to the king."

I did not know what else to do but weep outright and curse my own slothfulness; yet I dressed myself, but my page was ready long before me, and ran out of the chamber to see how affairs might yet stand. But he soon returned, and brought with him this joyful news, that indeed the time was not yet, but I had only overslept my breakfast, they being unwilling to awaken me because of my age.

But now it was time for me to go with him to the fountain where most of them were assembled. With this consolation my spirit returned again, so I was soon ready with my habit, and went after the page to the fountain in the aforementioned garden, where I found that the lion, instead of his sword, had a pretty large tablet by him. Now having looked well at it, I found that it was taken out of the ancient monuments, and placed here for some special honour. The inscription was somewhat worn out with age, and therefore I have a mind to set it down here, as it is, and give everyone leave to consider it.

HERMES PRINCEPS
POST TOTAL ILLATA
GENERI HUMANO DAMNA
DEI CONSILIO
ARTISQUE ADMINICULO
MEDICINA SALUBRIS FACTUS
HEIC FLUO.
BIBAT EX ME QUI PROTEST, LAVET QUI VULT:
TURBET QUI AUDET:
BIBITE FRATRES, ET VIVITE

(Hermes the prince. After so many wounds inflicted on humankind, here by God's counsel and the help of the art flow I, a healing medicine. Let him drink me who can: let him wash who will: let him trouble me who dare: drink, brethren and live.)

This writing might well be read and understood, and may therefore suitably be placed here, because it is easier than any of the rest.

Now after we had first washed ourselves out of the fountain, and every man had taken a draught out of an entirely golden cup, we were once again to follow the virgin into the hall, and there put on new apparel, which was all of cloth of gold gloriously set out with flowers. There was also given to everyone another golden fleece, which was set about with precious stones, and various workmanship according to the utmost skill of each artisan. On it hung a weighty medal of gold, on which were figured the sun and moon in opposition; but on the other side stood this saying, "The light of the moon shall be as the light of the sun, and the light of the sun shall be seven times lighter than at present." But our former jewels were laid in a little casket, and committed to one of the waiters.

After this the virgin led us out in our order, where the musicians waited ready at the door, all apparelled in red velvet with white guards. After which a door (which I never saw open before) to the royal winding stairs was unlocked. There the virgin led us, together with the music, up three hundred and sixty-five stairs; there we saw nothing that was not of extremely costly workmanship, full of artifice; and the further we went, the more glorious still was the furniture, until at length at the top we came under a painted arch, where the sixty virgins attended us, all richly apparelled. Now as soon as they had bowed to us, and we, as well as we could, had returned our reverence, our musicians were sent away, and must go down the stairs again, the door being shut after them. After this a little bell was tolled; then in came in a beautiful virgin who brought everyone a wreath of laurel. But our virgins had branches given them.

Meanwhile a curtain was drawn up, where I saw the king and queen as they sat there in their majesty, and had not the duchess yesterday so faithfully warned me, I should have forgotten myself, and have equalled this unspeakable glory to heaven. For apart from the fact that the room glistened with gold and precious stones, the queen's robes were moreover made so that I was not able to behold them. And whereas before I esteemed anything to be handsome, here all things so much surpassed the rest, as the stars in heaven are elevated.

In the meantime the virgin came in, and so each of the virgins taking one of us by the hand, with most profound reverence presented us to the king, whereupon the virgin began to speak thus: "That to honour your Royal Majesties (most gracious King and Queen) these lords here present have ventured here in peril of body and life, your Majesties have reason to rejoice, especially since the greatest part are qualified for the enlarging of your Majesties' estates and empire, as you will find by a most gracious and particular examination of each of them. Herewith I desired to have them presented in humility to your Majesties, with most humble suit to discharge myself of this commission of mine, and most graciously to take sufficient information from each of them, concerning both my actions and omissions."

Hereupon she laid down her branch upon the ground. Now it would have been very fitting for one of us to have put in and said something on this occasion, but seeing we were all tongue-tied, at length the old Atlas stepped forward and spoke on the king's behalf: "Their Royal Majesties do most graciously rejoice at your arrival, and wish that their royal grace be assured to all, and every man. And with your administration, gentle virgin, they are most graciously satisfied, and accordingly a royal reward shall therefore be provided for you. Yet it is still their intention that you shall also continue to be with them this day, inasmuch as they have no reason to mistrust you."

Hereupon the virgin humbly took up the branch again. And so we for the first time were to step aside with our virgin. This room was square on the front, five times broader than it was long; but towards the west it had a great arch like a porch, wherein in a circle stood three glorious royal thrones, yet the middlemost was somewhat higher than the rest. Now in each throne sat two persons. In the first sat a very ancient king with a grey beard, yet his consort was extraordinarily fair and young. In the third throne sat a black king of middle age, and by him a dainty old matron, not crowned, but covered with a veil. But in the middle sat the two young persons, and though they had likewise wreaths of laurel upon their heads, yet over them hung a large and costly crown. Now although they were not at this time so fair as I had before imagined to myself, yet so it was to be. Behind them on a round form sat for the most part ancient men, yet none of them had any sword or other weapon about him, at which I wondered. Neither saw I any other bodyguard, but certain virgins who were with us the day before, who sat on the sides of the arch.

Here I cannot pass over in silence how the little Cupid flew to and fro there, but for the most part he hovered over and played the wanton about the great crown; sometimes he seated himself between the two lovers, somewhat smiling upon them with his bow. Indeed, sometimes he made as if he would shoot one of us. In brief, this knave was so full of his waggery, that we would not even spare the little birds which flew in multitudes up and down the room, but tormented them all he could. The virgins also had their pastimes with him, but whenever they could catch him, it was not so easy a matter for him to get from them again. Thus this little knave made all the sport and mirth.

Before the queen stood a small but inexpressibly curious altar, on which lay a book covered with black velvet, a little overlaid with gold. By this stood a small taper in an ivory candlestick. Now although it was very small, yet it burnt continually, and was such that had not Cupid, in sport, now and then puffed upon it, we could not have conceived it to be fire. By this stood a sphere or celestial globe, which turned clearly about by itself. Next to this, a small striking-clock, and by that was a little crystal pipe or syphon-fountain, out of which perpetually ran a clear blood-red liquor. And last of all there was a skull, or death's head; in this was a white serpent, who was of such a length that though she wound about the rest of it in a circle, her tail still remained in one of the eyeholes until her head again entered the other; so she never stirred from her skull, unless it happened that Cupid twitched a little at her, for then she slipped in so suddenly that we all could not choose but marvel at it.

Together with this altar, there were up and down the room wonderful images, which moved themselves as if they had been alive, and had so strange a contrivance that it would be impossible for me to relate it all. Likewise, as we were passing out, there began such a marvellous kind of vocal music, that I could not tell for sure whether it was performed by the virgins who still stayed behind, or by the images themselves. Now we being satisfied for the time being, went away with our virgins, who (the musicians being already present) led us down the winding stairs again, and the door was diligently locked and bolted.

As soon as we had come again into the hall, one of the virgins began: "I wonder, sister, that you dare hazard yourself amongst so many people."

"My sister," replied our president, "I am afraid of none so much as of this man," pointing at me.

This speech went to my heart, for I well understood that she mocked at my age, and indeed I was the oldest of them all. Yet she comforted me again with the promise that if I behaved myself well towards her, she would easily rid me of this burden.

Meantime a light meal was again brought in, and everyone's virgin seated by him; they knew well how to shorten the time with handsome discourses, but what their discourses and sports were I dare not blab out of school. But most of the questions were about the arts, whereby I could easily gather that both young and old were conversant in knowledge. But still it ran in my thoughts how I might become young again, whereupon I was somewhat sadder.

The virgin perceived this, and therefore began, "I bet anything, if I lie with him tonight, he shall be more pleasant in the morning."

Hereupon they all began to laugh, and although I blushed all over, yet I had to laugh too at my own ill-luck.

Now there was one there who had a mind to return my disgrace upon the virgin again, so he said, "I hope not only we, but the virgins themselves too, will bear witness on behalf of our brother, that our lady president has promised to be his bedfellow tonight."

"I should be well content with it," replied the virgin, "if I had no reason to be afraid of my sisters here; there would be no hold with them should I choose the best and handsomest for myself, against their will."

"My sister," began another, "we find by this that your high office doesn't make you proud; so if with your permission we might divide by lot the lords here present among us for bedfellows, you should with our good will have such a prerogative."

We let this pass for a jest, and again began to discourse together. But our virgin could not leave tormenting us, and therefore began again. "My lords, what about if we should let fortune decide which of us must lie together tonight?"

"Well," I said, "if it may not be otherwise, we cannot refuse such an offer."

Now because it was concluded to make this trial after the meal, we resolved to sit no longer at table, so we arose, and each one walked up and down with his virgin.

"No," said the virgin, "it shall not be so yet, but let us see how fortune will couple us," upon which we were separated.

But now first arose a dispute how the business should be carried out; but this was only a premeditated device, for the virgin instantly made the proposal that we should mix ourselves together in a ring, and that she beginning to count the seventh from herself, was to be content with the following seventh, whether it were a virgin, or a man. For our parts we were not aware of any craft, and therefore permitted it to be so; but when we thought we had mingled ourselves very well, the virgins nevertheless were so clever that each one knew her station beforehand. The virgin began to reckon; the seventh from her was another virgin, the third seventh a virgin likewise, and this happened so long till (to our amazement) all the virgins came forth, and none of us was hit. Thus we poor pitiful wretches remained standing alone, and were moreover forced to suffer ourselves to be jeered at, and to confess we were very handsomely tricked. In short, whoever had seen us in our order, might sooner have expected the sky to fall, than that it should never have come to our turn. With this our sport was at an end, and we had to satisfy ourselves with the virgin's waggery.

In the interim, the little wanton Cupid came in to us too. But we could not sport ourselves with him enough, because he presented himself on behalf of their royal majesties, and delivered us a health (from them) out of a golden cup, and had to call our virgins to the king, declaring also that he could at this time tarry no longer with them. So with a due return of our most humble thanks we let him fly off again.

Now because (in the interim) the mirth had begun to fall to my consort's feet – and the virgins were not sorry to see it – they quickly started up a civil dance, which I beheld with pleasure rather than taking part; for my mercurialists were so ready with their postures, as if they had long been of the trade. After a few dances our president came in again, and told us how the artists and students had offered themselves to their royal majesties, for their honour and pleasure, to act a merry comedy before their departure; and if we thought it good to be present at this, and to wait upon their royal majesties to the House of the Sun, it would be acceptable to them, and they would most graciously acknowledge it. Hereupon in the first place we returned our most humble thanks for the honour vouchsafed us; not only this, but moreover we most submissively tendered our humble service.

This the virgin related again, and presently brought word to attend their royal majesties (in our order) in the gallery, where we were soon led; and we did not stay long there, for the royal procession was just ready, yet without any music at all. The unknown duchess who was with us yesterday went in front, wearing a small and costly coronet, apparelled in white satin. She carried nothing but a small crucifix which was made of a pearl, and this very day wrought between the young king and his Bride. After her went the six aforementioned virgins in two ranks, who carried the king's jewels belonging to the little altar. Next to these came the three kings. The Bridegroom was in the midst of them in a plain dress, but in black satin, after the Italian fashion. He had on a small round black hat, with a little pointed black feather, which he courteously took off to us, so to signify his favour towards us. We bowed ourselves to him, as also to the first, as we had been instructed before. After the kings came the three queens, two of whom were richly dressed, but she in the middle was likewise all in black, and Cupid held up her train. After this, intimation was given to us to follow, and after us the virgins, till at last old Atlas brought up the rear.

In such procession, through many stately walks, we at length came to the House of the Sun, there next to the king and queen, upon a richly furnished scaffold, to behold the previously ordained comedy. We indeed, though separated, stood on the right hand of the kings, but the virgins stood on the left, except those to whom the royal ensigns were committed. To them was allotted their own place at the top of all. But the rest of the attendants had to stand below between the columns, and to be content with that.

Now because there are many remarkable passages in this comedy, I will not omit to go over it briefly.

First of all a very ancient king came on, with some servants; before his throne was brought a little chest, with mention being made that it was found upon the water. Now it being opened, there appeared in it a lovely baby, together with some jewels, and a small letter of parchment sealed and superscribed to the king, which the king therefore opened; and having read it, wept, and then declared to his servants how injuriously the king of the Moors had deprived his aunt of her country, and had extinguished all the royal seed even to his infant, with the daughter of which country he had now the intention of matching his son. Hereupon he swore to maintain perpetual enmity with the Moor and his allies, and to revenge this upon them; and with this he commanded that the child should be tenderly nursed, and to make preparation against the Moor. Now this provision, and the disciplining of the young lady (who after she had grown up a little was committed to an ancient tutor) took up all the first act, with many very fine and laudable sports besides.

In the interlude a lion and griffin were set at one another to fight, and the lion got the victory, which was also a pretty sight.

In the second act, the Moor, a very black treacherous fellow, came on too. He, having with vexation understood that his murder had been discovered, and that a little lady was craftily stolen from him too, began thereupon to consult how by stratagem he might be able to encounter so powerful an adversary; on which he was eventually advised by certain fugitives who fled to him because of a famine. So the young lady, contrary to everyone's expectations, fell again into his hands; he would have been likely to have caused her to be slain if he had not been wonderfully deceived by his own servants. Thus this act was concluded too, with a marvellous triumph of the Moor.

In the third act a great army of the king's party was raised against the Moor, and put under the conduct of an ancient valiant knight, who fell into the Moor's country, till at length he forcibly rescued the young lady from the tower, and apparelled her anew. After this in a trice they erected a glorious scaffold, and placed their young lady upon it. Presently twelve royal ambassadors came, amongst whom the aforementioned knight made a speech, alleging that the king his most gracious lord had not only delivered her from death earlier, and even caused her to be royally brought up until now (though she had not behaved herself altogether as became her). But moreover his royal majesty had, before others, elected her to be a spouse for the young lord his son, and most graciously desired that the said espousals might actually be executed, if they would be sworn to his majesty upon the following articles. Hereupon out of a patent he caused certain glorious conditions to be read, which if it were not too long, would be well worthy of being recounted here. In brief, the young lady took an oath inviolably to observe the same, returning thanks too in a most seemly way for such a high grace. Whereupon they began to sing to the praise of God, of the king, and the young lady, and so for the time being departed.

For sport, in the meantime, the four beasts of Daniel, as he saw them in the vision and as he described them at length, were brought in, all of which had its certain signification.

In the fourth act the young lady was again restored to her lost kingdom, and crowned, and for a while, in this array, conducted about the place with extraordinary joy. After this many and various ambassadors presented themselves, not only to wish her prosperity, but also to behold her glory. Yet it was not for long that she preserved her integrity, but soon began again to look wantonly about her, and to wink at the ambassadors and lords; in this she truly acted her part to the life. These manners of hers were soon known to the Moor, who would by no means neglect such an opportunity, and because her steward did not pay sufficient attention to her, she was easily blinded with great promises, so that she did not keep good confidence with her king, but privately submitted herself entirely to the disposal of the Moor. Hereupon the Moor made haste, and having (by her consent) got her into his hands, he gave her good words until all her kingdom had subjected itself to him. After which, in the third scene of this act, he caused her to be led forth, and first to be stripped stark naked, and then to be bound to a post upon a scurvy wooden scaffold, and well scourged, and at last sentenced to death. This was so woeful a spectacle, that it made the eyes of many run over. Hereupon like this, naked as she was, she was cast into prison, there to await her death, which was to be procured by poison, which actually did not kill her, but made her leprous all over. Thus this act was for the most part lamentable.

Between acts, they brought forth Nebuchadnezzar's image, which was adorned with all manner of arms, on the head, breast, belly, legs and feet, and the like, of which more shall be said in the future explanation.

In the fifth act the young king was told of all that had passed between the Moor and his future spouse; he first interceded with his father for her, entreating that she might not be left in that condition; which his father having agreed to, ambassadors were despatched to comfort her in her sickness and captivity, but yet also to make her see her inconsiderateness. But she still would not receive them, but consented to be the Moor's concubine, which was also done, and the young king was acquainted with it.

After this came a band of fools, each of which brought with him a cudgel; within a trice they made a great globe of the world, and soon undid it again. It was a fine sportive fantasy.

In the sixth act the young king resolved to do battle with the Moor, which was also done. And although the Moor was discomforted, yet all held the young king too to be dead. At length he came to himself again, released his spouse, and committed her to his steward and chaplain. The first of these tormented her greatly; then the tables were turned, and the priest was so insolently wicked that he had to be above all, until this was reported to the young king; who hastily despatched one who broke the neck of the priest's mightiness, and adorned the Bride in some measure for the nuptials.

After the act a vast artificial elephant was brought forth. He carried a great tower with musicians, which was also well pleasing to all. In the last act the Bridegroom appeared with such pomp as cannot be believed, and I was amazed how it was brought to pass. The Bride met him in similar solemnity, whereupon all the people cried out LONG LIVE THE BRIDEGROOM! LONG LIVE THE BRIDE! – so that by this comedy they also congratulated our king and queen in the most stately manner, which (as I well observed) pleased them most extraordinarily well.

At length they walked about the stage in this procession, till at last they began to sing altogether as follows:

> I
> This lovely time
> Brings much joy
> With the king's wedding,
> So sing you all
> That it resound
> And gladness be to him
> Who gives it to us.

II
The beauteous Bride
Whom we have long awaited
Shall be betrothed to him,
And we have won
Whereafter we did strive
O happy he
Who looks to himself.

III
The elders good
Are bidden now,
For long they were in care,
In honour multiply
That thousands arise
From your own blood.

After this thanks were returned, and the comedy was finished with joy, and the particular enjoyment of the royal persons, so (the evening also drawing near already) they departed together in their aforementioned order.

But we were to attend the royal persons up the winding stairs into the aforementioned hall, where the tables were already richly furnished, and this was the first time that we were invited to the king's table. The little altar was placed in the midst of the hall, and the six royal ensigns previously mentioned were laid upon it. At this time the young king behaved himself very graciously towards us, but yet he could not be heartily merry; although he now and then discoursed a little with us, yet he often sighed, at which the little Cupid only mocked, and played his waggish tricks. The old king and queen were very serious; only the wife of one of the ancient kings was gay enough, the reason for which I did not yet understand.

During this time, the royal persons took up the first table, at the second only we sat. At the third, some of the principal virgins placed themselves. The rest of the virgins, and men, all had to wait. This was performed with such state and solemn stillness that I am afraid to say very much about it. But I cannot leave untouched upon here, how all the royal persons, before the meal, attired themselves in snow-white glittering garments, and so sat down at the table. Over the table hung the great golden crown, the precious stones of which would have sufficiently illuminated the hall without any other light. However, all the lights were kindled at the small taper upon the altar; what the reason was I did not know for sure. But I took very good notice of this, that the young king frequently sent meat to the white serpent upon the little altar, which caused me to muse.

Almost all the prattle at this banquet was made by little Cupid, who could not leave us (and me, indeed, especially) untormented. He was perpetually producing some strange matter. However, there was no considerable mirth, all went silently on; from which I myself could imagine some great imminent peril. For there was no music at all heard; but if we were asked anything, we had to give short round answers, and so let it rest. In short, all things had so strange a face, that the sweat began to trickle down all over my body; and I am apt to believe that the most stout-hearted man alive would then have lost his courage.

Supper being now almost ended, the young king commanded the book to be reached him from the little altar. This he opened, and caused it once again to be propounded to us by an old man, whether we resolved to abide by him in prosperity and adversity; which we having consented to with trembling, he further had us asked, whether we would give him our hands on it, which, when we could find no evasion, had to be so. Hereupon one after another arose, and with his own hand wrote himself down in this book.

When this also had been performed, the little crystal fountain, together with a very small crystal glass, was brought near, out of which all the royal persons drank one after another. Afterwards it was held out to us too, and so to all persons; and this was called the Draught of Silence. Hereupon all the royal persons presented us their hands, declaring that if we did not now stick to them, we should nevermore from now on see them; which truly made our eyes run over. But our president engaged herself and promised a great deal on our behalf, which gave them satisfaction.

Meantime a little bell was tolled, at which all the royal persons became so incredibly bleak, that we were ready to despair utterly. They quickly took off their white garments again, and put on entirely black ones. The whole hall likewise was hung about with black velvet, the floor was covered with black velvet, with which also the ceiling above was overspread (all this being prepared beforehand). After that the tables were also removed, and all seated themselves round about upon the form, and we also put on black habits. In came our president again, who had before gone out, and she brought with her six black taffeta scarves, with which she bound the six royal persons' eyes. Now when they could no longer see, six covered coffins were immediately brought in by the servants, and set down in the hall; also a low black seat was placed in the middle. Finally, there came in a very coal-black, tall man, who bore in his hand a sharp axe.

Now after the old king had first been brought to the seat, his head was instantly whipped off, and wrapped in a black cloth; but the blood was received into a great golden goblet, and placed with him in this coffin that stood by; which, being covered, was set aside. Thus it went with the rest also, so that I thought it would at length have come to me too, but it did not. For as soon as the six royal persons were beheaded, the black man went out again; another followed after him, and beheaded him too just before the door, and brought back his head together with the axe, which were laid in a little chest. This indeed seemed to me a bloody wedding, but because I could not tell what was yet to happen, for the time being I had to suspend my understanding until I had further resolved things. For the virgin too, seeing that some of us were faint-hearted and wept, bid us be content.

"For," she said to us, "the life of these now stands in your hands, and if you follow me, this death shall make many alive."

With this she intimated that we should go to sleep, and trouble ourselves no further on their part, for they should be sure to have their due right. And so she bade us all goodnight, saying that she must watch the dead bodies this night. We did this, and were each of us conducted by our pages into our lodgings. My page talked with me of sundry and various matters (which I still remember very well) and gave me cause enough to admire his understanding. But his intention was to lull me to sleep, which at last I well observed; so I made as though I was fast asleep, but no sleep came into my eyes, and I could not put the beheaded out of my mind.

Now my lodging was directly over against the great lake, so that I could easily look upon it, the windows being near to the bed. About midnight, as soon as it had struck twelve, suddenly I saw a great fire on the lake, so out of fear I quickly opened the window to see what would become of it. Then from afar I saw seven ships making forward, which were all full of lights. Above each of them on the top hovered a flame that passed to and fro, and sometimes descended right down, so that I could easily judge that it must be the spirits of the beheaded. Now these ships gently approached land, and each of them had no more than one mariner. As soon as they had come to shore, I saw our virgin with a torch going towards the ship, after whom the six covered coffins were carried, together with the little chest, and each of them was secretly laid in a ship.

So I awakened my page too, who greatly thanked me, for, having run up and down a lot all day, he might have slept through this altogether, though he knew quite well about it. Now as soon as the coffins were laid in the ships, all the lights were extinguished, and the six flames passed back together over the lake, so that there was no more than one light in each ship for a watch. There were also some hundreds of watchmen who had encamped themselves on the shore, and sent the virgin back again into the castle; she carefully bolted everything up again, so that I could judge that there was nothing more to be done this night, but that we must await the day.

So we again took ourselves to rest. And I only of all my company had a chamber towards the lake, and saw this, so that now I was also extremely weary, and so fell asleep in my manifold speculations.

The Fourth Day: Commentary

On this day, the middle one in the series of seven, alchemy begins to play an important role. The alchemical (or alchymical as it was formerly called) process is clothed in the image of the death of the three royal couples who are later reborn in the new figures of king and queen. The remarkable circumstance in this process is that Christian Rosenkreutz and his companions form part of it. They are the "helpers" of Lady Alchimia who gives them instructions.

In part, the imagery of alchemy is the same as that in the Book of Revelation. In the chapter "Who is Christian Rosenkreutz?" we will come back to this relationship. The alchemists could be considered as precursors who tried to work toward the future state of humanity that is expressed in the imagination of the marriage of heaven and earth:

> And I saw a new heaven and a new earth. The former heaven and the former earth had passed away, and the sea was no more. And I also saw the holy city, the New Jerusalem. It descended from the heavenly world, out of the realm of the Godhead. In its beauty of form it was like a bride adorned for marriage. (Rev.21:1–3 *M*).

Alchemy similarly uses the image of the union of two different worlds, which may be called heaven and earth, king and queen, or bride and bridegroom. Current literature has given much attention to the similarities between the *Chymical Wedding* and the Mystical Wedding (though the similarities are limited), but less so to the parallels with alchemy. This aspect will receive special emphasis in the next few chapters.

One fundamental premise of alchemy is the art of uniting the highest with the lowest in the right manner. In a certain sense, that is a dangerous art. Service of Mammon, the crudest materialism, in a certain respect also unites the highest with the lowest, but in such a way that the spiritual disappears and the soul loses itself in deadly, monotonous work. Spirit and soul are "invested" in matter. Rudolf Steiner wrote in the verse "Darkness, Light, Love":

> To bind oneself to matter
> Means to grind the soul to dust.
> To find oneself in spirit
> Means to unite human beings.
> To behold oneself in man
> Means to build worlds.[1]

Three different "marriages" are described in this verse: the union with darkness (matter), light (spirit), and the human being through love.

The alchemists follow the fundamental Hermetic law which begins as follows in the alchemical text *Tabula Smaragdina:* "True it is, without falsehood, certain and most true. That which is above is like that which is below..."[2] The anonymous author CVH describes the fundamental Hermetic law with the words: "It is a great science to unite the highest with the lowest and the lowest with the highest."[3]

This ostensibly simple law is radically different from a certain form of Christianity that was dominant for a long time. The contrast between the two was demonstrated one day when a student wanted to discuss the principles of the fundamental Hermetic law with a professor of theology. The latter was shocked and reacted with the words: "What are you doing now? You are pulling the Lord from his throne!"

This is the central problem that, for instance, brings the mystic Jakob Böhme into conflict with traditional Christianity. During his last ecclesiastical trial Böhme is told by his inquisitor Georg Richter: "This cobbler teaches that God resides in the human being! In the sinful, troubled human being! He says that nature is one with God! Isn't that enough? God will not let anyone take his eternity away from him!" He is accused of these heretical statements. In this notorious trial these two aspects of Christianity squarely face each other.

For the alchemists it is of the utmost importance to come to know the spiritual world on the earth in all its manifestations, and to recognise it in matter, in the transformations undergone by matter (alchemy), and in nature – in brief, in the Book of the World *(Liber Mundi).*

When we review the events of the fourth, fifth and sixth days we are hardly able to distinguish whether what is related is a spiritual or

Figure 6. Illustration from Michael Maier, Symbola aureae mensae duodecim nationum, *Frankfurt 1617.*

material process, an inner or an outer world. In his description of the sixth day Rudolf Steiner wrote: "... a path of knowledge that can penetrate the material basis of the soul life and receive the being of the spirit. To be able to effect this, one must be able to shed spiritual light upon this material basis."[4] All three elements mentioned in the above-quoted verse – darkness (matter), light (spirit), love (of the soul) – are united in the alchemical process.

One could even call the alchemist a "materialist," but in the original, more favourable sense of the word. The word "matter" comes from the Latin mater, mother. The alchemist knew that underlying matter there is a spiritual being that can be viewed as the mother of creation.* He would literally prostrate himself before this being from whom all matter came forth. The table in his laboratory became an altar. In old pictures we can see the alchemist standing at an altar as a priest (Figure 6).

* In the twelfth-century School of Chartres, Natura was also described as a feminine goddess.

The alchemist, however, did not simply accept the material world as it has become, but he brought the elements into processes and meditatively witnessed this chemistry. He became one with these processes. An alchemical document relates that at the moment of the transformation of a substance the alchemist sees a multi-coloured being emerging from it. This is obviously invisible to the external eye, but he observes with clairvoyant capacities how certain spiritual forces come into existence.*[5]

While in the early twentieth century most current scientific literature dismissed alchemy as a fraud, Steiner and Jung, independently of each other and by different methods, discovered that western alchemy was a Christian path of initiation. It is not, as some people continue to assert, only a hermetic path of initiation based on pre-Christian, Hermetic wisdom. Hermes Trismegistus is viewed as the great teacher and initiate of the Egyptian culture. He taught humanity that the physical world is the "handwriting" of the divine world: the hermetic fundamental law. He is also the one who taught humanity to value the physical world at its true worth, something that was not common in those days. One could call this hermetic, pre-Christian wisdom, "birth-wisdom" – knowledge that human beings brought with them out of the world of their origin. On the other hand, one could call alchemy "resurrection-wisdom." It owes its origin to Egyptian sources, but directs itself specifically to the future, the New Jerusalem. There is more about this in the descriptions of the fifth day, when this future creation is expressed in imagery.

The fourth day has a rather unfortunate beginning. Christian Rosen-kreutz consciously follows a slow path – but that he oversleeps is not quite his intention! "I did not know what else to do but weep outright and curse my own slothfulness." The others had not woken him on account of his age. On the one hand, his age helps him; he has more experience than the others. But it also leads to repeated teasing and mockery. As usual, he is the last to join the group. Upon arrival in the garden he sees the same lion that was tamed the previous day, now

* In *Das Silber und der Mond,* Lili Kolisko (1889–1976) refers to the alchemist Zosimos who saw rising up out of his altar a "copper-man," who was transformed into a "silver-man" and finally into a "gold-man."

holding a sign. The date at the bottom of the sign signifies the year of Christian Rosenkreutz's birth (1378) as mentioned in the *Confessio*. The text of the sign, which quotes Hermes, refers to the fall into sin ("so many wounds inflicted on humankind") and the healing thereof ("here by ... the help of the art flow I, a healing medicine ... drink, brethren and live"). The *chymical wedding*, which is drawing near, transfigures the body and heals it from the consequences of the fall. True alchemists began their process with meditation on what they called the "virginal earth" – the creation as it once was before the fall into sin. Subsequently, they went through all kinds of alchemical processes, in seven phases which we will encounter in the *Chymical Wedding*, ending with what they called *materia ultima*, or the Philosopher's Stone. While working with, and meditating on, matter they would develop their inner life, so that they would make a step toward the realisation of this future creation, "a new heaven and a new earth."

At the beginning of this path, Christian Rosenkreutz and the others have to wash themselves and drink from the fountain of Hermes; then they receive new, gold-coloured clothes. The new golden fleece which they also receive indicates the image of the future to which the alchemist strove: "The light of the moon shall be as the light of the sun, and the light of the sun shall be seven times lighter than at present.." In the book of Isaiah (30:26) we find the exact same text, but there it is followed by the words: "... in the day when the LORD binds up the hurt of his people, and heals the wounds inflicted by his blow." It is a remarkable parallel with the above-quoted words of Hermes – a healing that is not fully complete until the creation that St John calls the New Jerusalem in the Book of Revelation, but is to a certain extent prepared by alchemy.[6]

After the opening of a door – remember the dream at the end of the third day – they continue on their way. Now the path is no longer horizontal or into the depths, but for the first time it goes up along a spiral stair with 365 steps. Step by step – just as the way of alchemy is a work of patience. We could also say: we only reach the spiritual world if, on every one of the 365 days of the year, we exert ourselves for it.

Upon the group's arrival upstairs the king and queen are revealed. The previous day they were still hidden behind a curtain; now they are unveiled in indescribable splendour. The virgin Alchimia is charged to continue assisting them on the path. In the apse of the hall three thrones are standing on which three royal couples are seated. In the imaginative world "one" can suddenly become "three", just like the three soul forces separate as soon as a human being enters the spiritual world.[7]

"They were not at this time so fair as I had before imagined to myself, yet so it was to be," says Christian Rosenkreutz about the three royal pairs. It is as if the picture of the future, the king and queen in their "unspeakable glory," is taken down a notch in the reality of the moment. Christian Rosenkreutz looks at himself in his own mirror as it were, and sees the three soul forces in the form of the king with the grey beard and his young spouse (thinking), the black king and his veiled wife (the will), and in the middle the young royal pair with the laurel wreaths (feeling). Later we will see that these royal pairs and their fortunes have everything to do with Christian Rosenkreutz. (The fact that the masculine and feminine, king and queen, are present in every human being hardly needs to be mentioned today.)

Right here a little tease appears on the scene, who leaves his traces everywhere, just when things are becoming serious! Everywhere he goes, little Cupid – herald of the goddess Venus who will play a role the next day – spreads joy and well-being, the most carefree forms of love.

In front of the queen stands an altar with six attributes: a black velvet book, a candle in an ivory candlestick, a celestial globe, a little clock, a tiny crystal fountain with blood-red water, and a skull with a white snake. The celestial globe reflects the cosmos in miniature ("As above, so below"). The clock indicates that what occurs on earth has to be in harmony with the laws of the cosmos (we derive our time from the cosmos). The fountain with blood-red water and the skull with the white snake symbolise the opposite worlds of life and death. The alchemists studied what one could call life in death and death in life. The white snake that crawls into and out of the skull, but never all the way out, is an imagination of this.

When the group has gone back down again they become the butt of the merriment of the maidens. The conversation at table is about the arts; that is, the art of alchemy. Christian Rosenkreutz is teased with his age, and would very much like to be young again. Lady Alchimia proposes that he share her bed with her that night.

In alchemy that is literally known as the *"chymical wedding-*bed". The Philosopher's Stone not only heals, it also rejuvenates – hence Christian Rosenkreutz's wish. Here it seems like just a word game that ends up with the men cutting a pretty foolish figure: "we had to satisfy ourselves with the virgin's waggery." Christian Rosenkreutz prefers to sit down and watch the dance of his mercurial friends (they had washed in the fountain of Mercury/Hermes) with the maidens. Apparently he is thinking about other things.

In the House of the Sun an odd comedy is staged in honour of the king. We see the entire drama of the origin of the human soul as in a nutshell, the entanglement in the material world and the appeal of the heavenly world calling the soul to return to its original destiny. In seven images the drama of the development of humanity is put on the stage. One of the leading parts is that of the Moor who abducts the virgin – the human soul – binds her hand and foot and threatens to kill her.

When the virgin has been liberated from the tower of the Moor, she is told that the king has destined her to marry his beloved son. The divine Father does not abandon the human soul but has destined her for marriage with the Son, the Saviour.

In an interlude the four beasts from the vision in the Book of Daniel (7:3ff) are shown. These are the opposing powers of which the book says: "He shall speak words against the Most High, and shall wear out the saints of the Most High, and shall think to change the times and the law; and they shall be given into his hand for a time, two times, and half a time" (Dan.7:25). A future is described in this Old Testament Apocalypse in which, under the influence of the four beasts, human beings radically turn away from the divine world for a span of time equal to the three and a half days of the ancient forms of initiation: "a time, two times and half a time." Thus in the next, fourth, act the virgin also forgets her destiny, is overpowered by the Moor, thrown into a dungeon and stricken by leprosy.*

---

* Here we can see some parallels with Monostatos, the Moor in Mozart's opera
The Magic Flute. In *The Magic Flute: an Alchemical Allegory,* van den Berk describes this
entire opera as an alchemical process ending in the marriage of Tamino and Pamina.
The author had discovered a document by an anonymous Italian author dating back to
1816, in which all the characters are compared with alchemical symbols.

In the next interlude the image of Nebuchadnezzar appears of whom the Bible says: "The head of this image was of fine gold, its breast and arms of silver, its belly and thighs of bronze, its legs of iron, its feet partly of iron and partly of clay." (Dan.2:32f) It is the familiar picture of feet of clay, an Old Testament analogy of the succession of cultures, their progressive profanity (from "gold" to "clay") and decadence.

In the fifth act the son becomes concerned about the virgin who has now allied herself with the Moor and has forgotten her calling. In another interlude "came a band of fools, each of which brought with him a cudgel; within a trice they made a great globe of the world, and soon undid it again. It was a fine sportive fantasy."

The seven acts of the play represent the seven cultural epochs of humanity as described by anthroposophy. In our fifth cultural epoch we are familiar with this "entertaining fantasy": it is the work of materialistic science, which produces a second creation. "Everything" can be made – only the spiritual bond, that connects living beings with each other, is lacking. It is like a world on its own that is "made," and just as quickly falls apart again.

In the sixth act the evil is undone: the young king, the son, kills the Moor and liberates his bride who then prepares for the wedding. The interlude shows a merry scene: "a vast artificial elephant was brought forth. He carried a great tower with musicians, which was also well pleasing to all." Maybe this is the picture of the carrying forces of life (the elephant carrying a burden), that are at the same time the carriers of the "inaudible music" of the creation, the harmonies of the spheres.

Just like the Book of Revelation, this performance also ends with a "heavenly" wedding. Alchemy uses eloquent images for this dramatic transition from darkness to light. One of these shows a "swamp man" (Figure 7). A jet-black man stands in the mud stretching out one arm that turns white toward the hand. At the edge of the swamp stands an angel who hands the man a garment – a striking and simple image showing how matter remains dark and dead if it is not "taken in hand," and cultivated. When the material world is opened again to the spirit, when angel forces permeate the natural world, matter is cleansed of the consequences of the fall into sin and finds its destiny. In the picture we see the swamp man, who reaches out to the angelic world, longing for

Figure 7. The swamp man. Detail from Splendor Solis *manuscript.*

redemption. In the drama it is the Moor who makes matter heavy and kills it, and who would suffocate the human soul – if we should leave creation to its fate.

St Paul expresses it as follows:

> All around us creation waits with great longing that the sons of God shall begin to shine forth in mankind. Creation has become transitory, not through its own doing, but because of him who, becoming transitory himself, dragged it down with him, and therefore everything in it is full of longing for the future. For the breath of freedom will also waft through the kingdoms of creation; the tyranny of transitory existence will cease. When the sphere of the Spirit grows bright, unfreedom will be replaced by the freedom which is intended for all God's offspring. We know that the whole of creation suffers and sighs in the pangs of a new birth until the present day. And not creation alone; although we have received the first fruits of the new Spirit, we, too, are painfully waiting for the secret of sonship which is to bring redemption right into our bodily nature. (Rom.8:19–23 *M).*

The alchemists called the first of the seven phases mortification, the condition of death. They meditated on the process of death, and the soul mood they then experienced was *melancholy.* This is also the mood the soul goes through when one meditates on the way of the passion in the sense of the *Imitatio Christi.* It is a necessary condition if it is one's intention later to become a participant in the resurrection. "Unless a grain of wheat dies when it falls into the earth, it remains as it is. But if it dies, it bears much fruit." (Jn.12:24 *M).*

It may appear strange that this stage occurs on the fourth day, the day of Easter. Precisely on the day of the resurrection of Christ, Christian Rosenkreutz goes through his death experience. This may not be without meaning, however, for the way of the imitation of Christ could not be opened until after his resurrection – "the beginning of the new life among the souls who have fallen asleep" (1Cor.15:20 *M).* In a delicate way the virgin expresses the prospect of the resurrection at the end of this day: "if you follow me, this death shall make many alive."

In a mood of melancholy and earnestness the king asks the "mercurialists" to pledge fidelity to him and to confirm it by their signatures. The white royal robes are exchanged for black velvet, with which the entire hall is also draped from the ceiling to the floor. At the time of the *Chymical Wedding* (1459) velvet was made of silk, a material that comes from a transformation, a metamorphosis: the work of the silkworm. Appropriately, in alchemy the first of the seven stages is sometimes called *nigredo,* black.

Then follows the "bloody wedding," the beheading of the three royal pairs by a "coal-black" man, who is subsequently also beheaded by an eighth person. When the poet Goethe read the *Chymical Wedding* he was so appalled by these bloody scenes that he was inspired to create something entirely new. He wrote to Frau Von Stein: "I read the *Chymical Wedding* of Christian Rosenkreutz to the end. I can tell a nice fairytale some time when it is reborn. In its old form it is impossible to enjoy." In 1795 he wrote the *Fairytale of the Green Snake and the Beautiful Lily,* in which the *Chymical Wedding* comes to life again in different imagery.

Christian Rosenkreutz is connected heart and soul with the beheaded royal pairs and their further fortunes. The virgin clearly expresses this: "the life of these now stands in your hands." While she has to keep watch with the dead, the "mercurialists" are taken to their sleeping quarters. Apparently, Christian Rosenkreutz is the only one who keeps his promise: "no sleep came into my eyes, and I could not put the beheaded out of my mind." In a certain sense he remains true to the dead. He draws the consequences of his self-chosen destiny, which he has confirmed with his signature, and he stays awake. He "adds value" again to a crucial event, but he also experiences something extraordinary.

Now my lodging was directly over against the great lake, so that I could easily look upon it ... About midnight, as soon as it had struck twelve, suddenly I saw a great fire on the lake, so out of fear I quickly opened the window to see what would become of it. Then from afar I saw seven ships making forward, which were all full of lights. Above each of them on the top hovered a flame that passed to and fro, and sometimes descended right down, so that I could easily judge that it must be the spirits of the beheaded.

Christian Rosenkreutz is the only one who witnesses that the six covered coffins and the chest with the head of the Moor are put on board. He confides his discovery to the page who accompanies him and who has slept through the event.

In the original edition of the *Chymical Wedding* the little word *Ich* (I) stands in this critical spot, capitalised in the middle of the sentence: "suddenly I saw a great fire on the lake." This is most unusual in German; it is as if the author wished to call attention to something extraordinary. Nowhere else is the word *ich* capitalised in the original edition.

The path of initiation is a path of unremitting sacrifice. The human being has to sacrifice everything he has made his own in life. The Christian path of initiation of the Rosicrucians and alchemists was one that led through the depths of the experience of death, but also of matter. The Rosicrucian had to go though these experiences in all intensity, in order to receive out of the death of matter the power of the resurrection. The sign of the Rosicrucians expresses both of these experiences: the black cross with the seven red roses. For this reason Christian Rosenkreutz's path begins during Passion Week and ends after Easter. The sign on the letter he receives on the first day – "In this sign + you shall overcome" – becomes reality.

The Fifth Day

The Fifth Day

The night was over, and the dear wished-for day broken, when hastily I got out of bed, more desirous to learn what might yet ensue, than that I had slept enough. Now after I had put on my clothes, and according to my custom had gone down the stairs, it was still too early, and I found nobody else in the hall; so I entreated my page to lead me about a little in the castle, and show me something rare. He was now (as always) willing, and led me down certain steps under ground, to a great iron door, on which the following words in great copper letters were fixed:

(Here lies buried Venus, that beauty which has undone many a great man both in fortune, honour, blessing and prosperity.)

This I copied, and set down in my table-book. Now after this door was opened, the page led me by the hand through a very dark passage, till we came again to a very little door, that was now ajar; for (as my page informed me) it was first opened yesterday when the coffins were taken out, and had not since been shut. Now as soon as we stepped in, I saw the most precious thing that nature ever created, for this vault had no light other than that from certain huge great garnets, and this (as I was informed) was the king's treasury. But the main and most glorious thing that I saw here was a sepulchre (which stood in the middle) so rich that I wondered that it was not better guarded. To which the page answered me, that I had good reason to be thankful to my stars, by whose influence it was that I had now seen certain pieces which no other human eye (except the king's family) had ever had a view of.

This sepulchre was triangular, and had in the middle of it a vessel of polished copper; the rest was of pure gold and precious stones. In the vessel stood an angel, who held in his arms an unknown tree, which continually dropped fruit into the vessel; and as often as the fruit fell into the vessel, it turned into water, and ran out from there into three small golden vessels standing by. This little altar was supported by these three animals, an eagle, an ox and a lion, which stood on an exceedingly costly base.

I asked my page what this might signify.

"Here," he said, "lies buried Lady Venus, that beauty which has undone many a great man, both in fortune, honour, blessing and prosperity." After which he showed me a copper door on the pavement.

"Here," he said, "if you please, we may go further down."

"I am still following you," I replied.

So I went down the steps, where it was exceedingly dark, but the page immediately opened a little chest, in which stood a small ever-burning taper, at which he kindled one of the torches which lay by. I was greatly terrified, and seriously asked how he dared do this.

He said by way of answer "As long as the royal persons are still at rest, we have nothing to fear."

Then I saw a rich bed ready made, hung about with curious curtains, one of which he drew aside, where I saw the Lady Venus stark naked (for he heaved up the coverlets too) lying there in such beauty, and in such a surprising fashion, that I was almost beside myself; neither do I yet know whether it was a piece thus carved, or a human corpse that lay dead there. For she was altogether immovable, and yet I dared not touch her. So she was again covered, and the curtain drawn before her, yet she was still (as it were) in my eye. But I soon saw behind the bed a tablet on which it was written as follows:

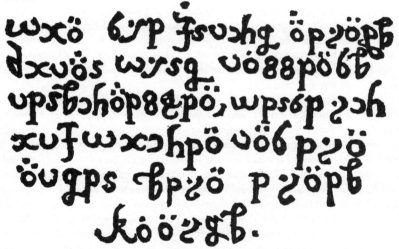

(When the fruit of my tree shall be quite melted down then I shall awake and be the mother of a king.)

I asked my page about this writing, but he laughed, with the promise that I should know it too. So, he putting out the torch, we ascended again. Then I had a better look at all the little doors, and first found that on every corner there burned a small taper of pyrites, of which I had before taken no notice, for the fire was so clear that it looked much more like a stone than a taper. From this heat the tree was forced continually to melt, yet it still produced new fruit. Now behold (said the page) what I heard revealed to the king by Atlas. When the tree (he said) shall be quite melted down, then shall Lady Venus awake, and be the mother of a king.

Whilst he was thus speaking, in flew the little Cupid, who at first was somewhat abashed at our presence, but seeing us both look more like the dead than the living, he could not in the end refrain from laughing, demanding what spirit had brought us there. I with trembling answered him, that I had lost my way in the castle, and had come here by chance, and that the page likewise had been looking up and down for me, and at last came upon me here, and I hoped he would not take it amiss.

"Well then, that's well enough yet, my old busy grandsire," said Cupid, "but you might easily have served me a scurvy trick, had you been aware of this door. Now I must look better to it," and so he put a strong lock on the copper door where we had before descended.

I thanked God that he had not come upon us sooner. My page too was happier, because I had helped him so well in this pinch.

"Yet," said Cupid, "I cannot let it pass unrevenged that you were so near stumbling upon my dear mother."

With that he put the point of his dart into one of the little tapers, and heating it a little, pricked me with it on the hand, which at that time I paid little attention to, but was glad that it had gone so well for us, and that we came off without further danger.

Meantime my companions had got out of bed too, and had returned into the hall again. To them I also joined myself, making as if I had just risen. After Cupid had carefully made all fast again, he came to us too, and would have me show him my hand, where he still found a little drop of blood; at which he heartily laughed, and bade the rest have a care of me, as I would shortly end my days. We all wondered how Cupid could be so merry, and have no sense at all of yesterday's sad occurrences. But he was in no way troubled.

Now our president had in the meantime made herself ready for the journey, entering all in black velvet, yet she still carried her branch of laurel. Her virgins too had their branches. Now all things being ready, the virgin asked us first to drink something, and then presently to prepare for the procession, so we did not tarry long but followed her out of the hall into the court. In the court stood six coffins, and my companions thought nothing other than that the six royal persons lay in them, but I well observed the device. Yet I did not know what was to be done with these others. By each coffin were eight muffled men. Now as soon as the music began (it was so mournful and doleful a tune, that I was astonished at it) they took up the coffins, and we (as we were ordered) had to go after them into the aforementioned garden, in the middle of which was erected a wooden edifice, having round about the roof a glorious crown, and standing upon seven columns. Within it were formed six sepulchres, and by each of them was a stone; but in the middle was a round hollow rising stone. In these graves the coffins were quietly and with many ceremonies laid. The stones were shovelled over them, and they shut fast. But the little chest was to lie in the middle.

Herewith my companions were deceived, for they imagined nothing other but that the dead corpses were there. Upon the top of all there was a great flag, having a phoenix painted on it, perhaps the more to delude us. Here I had great occasion to thank God that I had seen more than the rest.

Now after the funerals were done, the virgin, having placed herself upon the midmost stone, made a short oration, that we should be constant to our engagements, and not repine at the pains we were hereafter to undergo, but be helpful in restoring the present buried royal persons to life again; and therefore without delay to rise up with her, to journey to the Tower of Olympus, to fetch from there medicines useful and necessary for this purpose.

This we soon agreed to, and followed her through another little door right to the shore. There the seven aforementioned ships stood all empty, on which the virgins stuck up their laurel branches, and after they had distributed us in the six ships, they caused us thus to begin our voyage in God's name, and looked upon us as long as they could have us in sight, after which they, with all the watchmen, returned into the castle. Our ships each had a great flag with a peculiar device. Five of them indeed had the five *Corpora Regularia,** each their own, but mine, in which the virgin sat too, carried a globe. Thus we sailed on in a particular order, each having only two crewmen. Foremost was the ship *A* in which in my opinion the Moor lay. In this were twelve musicians, who played excellently well, and its device was a pyramid. Next followed three abreast, *B, C,* and *D,* in which we were. I sat in *C.*

In the middle behind these came the two fairest and stateliest ships, *E* and *F,* stuck about with many branches of laurel, having no passengers in them; their flags were the sun and moon. But in the rear was only one ship, *G;* in this were forty virgins.

Now having passed over this lake in this way, we first went through a narrow arm, into the right seas, where all the sirens, nymphs, and sea-goddesses were waiting for us; wherefore they immediately dispatched a sea-nymph to us to deliver their present and offering of honour to the wedding. It was a costly, great set pearl, the like of which has never been seen, neither in our world nor yet in the new world. Now the virgin having kindly received it, the nymph further entreated that audience might be given to their entertainments, and to make a little stand, which the virgin was content to do, and commanded the two great ships to stand in the middle, and the rest to encompass them in a pentagon.

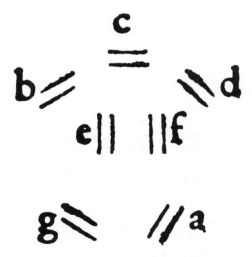

* The five regular planets Saturn, Mars, Earth, Venus and Mercury.

After which the nymphs fell into a ring about, and with a most delicate sweet voice began to sing as follows:

I

Naught better is on earth
Than lovely noble love
Whereby we be as God
And no one vexes his neighbour.
So let unto the king be sung
That all the sea shall sound.
We ask, and answer you.

II

What has to us life brought?
'Tis Love
Who has brought grace again?
'Tis Love
Whence are we born?
Of Love
How were we all forlorn?
Without Love

III

Who has us then begotten?
'Twas Love
Wherefore were we suckled?
For Love
What owe we to our elders?
'Tis Love
And why are they so patient?
From Love.

IV

What do all things o'ercome?
'Tis Love
Can we find Love as well?
Through Love
Where does good work appear?
In Love
Who can unite a pair?
'Tis Love.

V

So let us all sing
That it resound
To honour Love

Which will increase
With our lord king and queen,
Their bodies are here, their souls are fled.

VI
And as we live
So shall God give
Where love and grace
Did sunder them
That we with flame of Love
May haply join them up again.

VII
So shall this song
In greatest joy
Though thousand generations come
Return into eternity.

When they, with most admirable concert and melody, had finished this song, I no more wondered at Ulysses for stopping the ears of his companions, for I seemed to myself the most unhappy man alive, because nature had not made me, too, so trim a creature. But the virgin soon dispatched them, and commanded us to set sail from there; so the nymphs went off too, after they had been presented with a long red scarf for a gratuity, and dispersed themselves in the sea.

I was at this time aware that Cupid began to work with me too, which yet tended by a very little towards my credit, and forasmuch as my giddiness is not likely to be beneficial to the reader, I am resolved to let it rest as it is. But this was the very wound that in the first book I received on the head in a dream. And let everyone take warning by me of loitering about Venus' bed, for Cupid can by no means brook it.

After some hours, having gone a good way in friendly discourses, we came within sight of the Tower of Olympus, so the virgin commanded to give the signal of our approach by the discharge of some pieces, which was also done. And immediately we saw a great white flag thrust out, and a small gilded pinnace sent forth to meet us. Now as soon as this had come to us, we perceived in it a very ancient man, the warden of the tower, with certain guards clothed in white, by whom we were cordially received, and so conducted to the tower.

This tower was situated upon an island which was exactly square, and which was environed with a wall that was so firm and thick that I myself counted two hundred and sixty paces over. On the other side of the wall was a fine meadow with certain little gardens, in which grew strange, and to me unknown, fruits; and then again there was an inner wall about the tower. The tower itself was just as if seven round towers had been built one by another, yet the midmost was somewhat the higher, and within they all entered one into another, and had seven storeys one above another. Having come in this way to the gates of the tower, we were led a little aside by the wall, so that, as I well observed, the coffins might be brought into the tower without our taking notice; of this the rest knew nothing.

This being done, we were conducted into the tower at the very bottom, which although it was excellently painted, yet we had little recreation there; for this was nothing but a laboratory, where we had to beat and wash plants, and precious stones, and all sorts of things, and extract their juice and essence, and put the same in glasses, and hand them over to be put aside. And truly our virgin was so busy with us, and so full of her directions, that she knew how to give each of us enough employment, so that in this island we had to be mere drudges, till we had achieved all that was necessary for the restoring of the beheaded bodies.

Meantime (as I afterwards understood) three virgins were in the first apartment washing the bodies with all diligence. Now when we had at last almost finished this preparation of ours, nothing more was brought us but some broth with a little draught of wine, by which I well observed that we were not here for our pleasure. For when we had finished our day's work, too, everyone had only a mattress laid on the ground for him, with which we were to content ourselves.

For my part I was not very much bothered about sleeping, and therefore walked out into the garden, and at length came as far as the wall; and because the heaven was at that time very clear, I could well drive away the time in contemplating the stars. By chance I came to a great pair of stone stairs, which led up to the top of the wall. And because the moon shone very bright, I was so much the more confident, and went up, and looked a little upon the sea too, which was now exceedingly calm.

And thus having good opportunity to consider more about astronomy, I found that this present night there would occur a conjunction of the planets, the like of which was not otherwise usually to be observed. Now having looked a good while at the sea, and it being just about midnight, as soon as it had struck twelve I saw from afar the seven flames passing over the sea towards here, and taking themselves towards the top of the spire of the tower. This made me somewhat afraid, for as soon as the flames had settled themselves, the winds arose, and began to make the sea very tempestuous. The moon also was covered with clouds, and my joy ended with such fear that I scarcely had enough time to find the stairs again, and take myself to the tower again. Now whether the flames tarried any longer, or passed away again, I cannot say, for in this obscurity I did not dare venture abroad more.

So I lay down on my mattress, and there being in the laboratory a pleasant and gently murmuring fountain, I fell asleep so much the sooner. And thus the fifth day too was concluded with wonders.

The Fifth Day: Commentary

On the fifth and sixth days it appears as if the story of the *Chymical Wedding* is becoming even more earthly, not only because of the description of all kinds of processes that we more or less recognise from our chemistry, but also because at the beginning of the fifth day the path goes into the depth, down a stairway into the earth. And the remarkable thing of these last days is that, once we begin to understand the language, they make it possible to look at the earth with different eyes. Not only did Rosicrucians and alchemists look at the world of matter differently from the way we do, they also worked with it in a very different manner. One could call the laboratories in which we investigate the material world torture chambers compared with the way the alchemists handled substances. In a certain sense we put matter on the rack in order to make it usable for our industrial and economic purposes.* We only need to look at the title and the author of a well-known alchemical work to realise what a world of difference there is between alchemy and our chemistry. Around 1412 an anonymous Franciscan, using the pseudonym of "He who has the nature of a virgin" wrote a book entitled *The Book of the Holy Trinity,* in which alchemy is described as a Christian path. Those who embarked on this path had to deal with matter in a "virginal" manner, as suggested by this author.

We also find religious contemplations on matter in movements that may be considered as offshoots of the old alchemy, such as early German theosophy. "Corporeality is the end of God's ways," wrote the German theologian and theosophist Friedrich Christoph Oetinger (1702–82).

According to many older views, matter is a creation of the highest spiritual powers. In the school of Dionysius the Areopagite, who brought the teaching of the celestial hierarchies, it was known that the highest hierarchies – the Thrones, Cherubim and Seraphim – laid the foundation for the creation of matter. According to several even older cosmologies, matter will at a time in a far distant future, reveal its true nature. In our creation, matter is always a veil, *maya,* as it is called

---

* It could be said that this way of working with matter was introduced by Francis Bacon (1561–1626), who was also the first to use the picture of the rack for his experimental methods. See also Heyer, *Geschichtsimpulse.*

in Indian teaching. But in a future state of development something entirely different will come forth from it. In anthroposophy these future phases of development are called Jupiter and Venus.[1] We will come across both names in the *Chymical Wedding*.

In many different cultures, cosmologies are taught that speak of several successive creations. In his book *Masked Gods* the anthropologist Frank Waters describes seven stages of evolution known to the Navajo Indians. In this series of seven the creation becomes ever more dense, until in the middle phase matter develops as we know it; subsequently it gradually spiritualises again.

Now, the alchemists studied the spiritual forces that lie at the foundation of nature, and that will be revealed in the phase of Venus mentioned above. All matter carries this Venus power, the power of love, in itself. From the moment when matter reveals its spiritual nature, one will no longer be able to speak of physical forces, because it will become evident that an incredible love is "invested" in what we call matter. One could say that the alchemists sought to connect themselves with these forces of love in a "virginal" manner. In silence and solitude they prepared themselves for these future Jupiter and Venus creations.

This search for the essence of matter also harbours a great danger. When we connect ourselves so deeply with material processes, we always run the risk that *maya,* illusion, will intrude in our consciousness in place of the underlying creative powers. Actually, that is what we – products of the age of materialism – do all the time: we are deceived by physical appearance, and have no notion of the forces we are handling on a daily basis.

Following this train of thought, we can also become more aware of the difference between genuine and false alchemy. The true alchemist always kept his inner eye on the spiritual force; that was for him the crux of the matter. The false alchemist lost himself in the *maya* of matter and went in search of physical gold. Rudolf Steiner wrote in his essay on the *Chymical Wedding*:

The moment the soul takes the alchemical path, it enters the region of spirit behind sense perception, and it falls into the vortex of illusion in which it can preserve its being only if

it brings out of its experience in the sense world a sufficient
capacity to distinguish error and truth. If it has not taken
the precaution to acquire such a capacity, then the whirl of
illusion will drive it into a world where it must become lost.[2]

In this connection, Rudolf Steiner characterises the path of
alchemy as the opposite of the path of mysticism. While alchemy is
the way out into the world and leads to union with the spirituality of
nature ("chymical wedding"), the path of mysticism leads into one's
own inner world, where the soul unites with one's higher spiritual
being ("mystical marriage"). The alchemist runs the risk of losing
himself. The danger for the mystic is that he concentrates his inner
consciousness of self to such an extent that he loses his relationship to
the world, and only experiences his own inner being. There is a story
about the mystic Bernard of Clairvaux (1090–1153) who was driven
along the Lake of Geneva in Switzerland for a whole day and in the
evening had no idea that the road had followed the edge of the water.

On the fifth day love plays the leading part in the appearance of
the goddess Venus. It is the only force human beings can take with
them across the threshold of the spiritual world, unchanged and
unhindered. Thinking has to be turned inside out so as to change
from earthly intellect to spiritual intelligence. Willpower cannot
realise itself in the spiritual world as it does on earth. But for the
power of the human middle region, love, there is no barrier between
these two worlds. Hence the important role love can play in our
relationships to the dead.

Friedrich Rittelmeyer, one of the founders of the Christian
Community, once had an remarkable experience in this regard. He
dreamed that he saw his mother, who had died years ago, sitting in
the window of the house in which he had grown up. In his dream,
Rittelmeyer walked up to the door to open it, but it remained closed.
His mother was standing on the other side, but she too was unable
to open the door – the portal of death, as it is sometimes called.
As he was holding the doorknob in his hand he felt in his dream
how a stream of love came to him. It was the love of the deceased
mother that reached him, completely unhindered. With this force still
palpably present he woke up.

This is an example of purely spiritual love. Things become more difficult when the material world plays a role in love. In alchemy it was permissible to occupy oneself with this only in a "virginal manner." What happens when this condition is not followed is demonstrated in the following event. Someone who had studied and worked with the *Chymical Wedding* for many years once had the following dream. He had to make his way through a mass of people. Left and right he saw the most attractive and lovely women he could imagine. With a certain effort he was able to make his way – until at the end of two long rows he saw the goddess Venus in all her dazzling beauty. "And then I did," the person told me, "what you should not do. I ran up to her and threw myself into her arms. The next moment I was smacked back onto the earth and woke up!" In this way we could imagine the temptation Christian Rosenkreutz now undergoes – a temptation, however, which he overcomes.

To conclude this introductory part, here is a description of a well-known mystic who did not stop with the inner experience, but also took the outward path and discovered these Venus-forces in material substance.

Jakob Böhme (1575–1624) relates that when he was 25 years old he had a wondrous vision of a pewter vase that was standing on his table. Suddenly, in the outer manifestation of this object the spiritual power appeared that underlay its existence. His biographer, Abraham von Franckenberg, wrote about this: "He went outside and was able to gaze, as it were, into the heart and the innermost nature of the world, which overwhelmed him with joy; he became very still and praised God." Böhme was so profoundly impressed by this experience that he did not speak for five months. He then wrote his book *Aurora.*

Steiner said about this that here was someone who described what in the old mysteries was called beholding the sun at midnight. At a certain stage of initiation, the human being becomes able to look straight through matter and behold how the sun penetrates with spiritual powers into the heart of the entire earth. However, such alchemical experiences are only possible when someone has the courage also to experience in his body the death forces that work in matter. In the alchemical work *Atalanta Fugiens* (1618) Michael Maier wrote: "The human being can in no other way be renewed and rejuvenated than by his death."

As Christian Rosenkreutz woke up late at the beginning of the fourth day, so he is now the early bird, and a good thing it is, for it gives him the opportunity to experience something the others sleep through. In the early morning his page shows him around in the castle.

As far as I know, in all the literature about the *Chymical Wedding* Rudolf Steiner is the first and only one who wonders why Christian Rosenkreutz is sometimes led by the virgin, then again by the page. He arrived at the following noteworthy answer: "where the personal will of the spiritual investigator makes its way, it is pictured ... by images of boys leading the way."[3] Whenever Christian Rosenkreutz wants to do something, or when he is just curious about something, he needs his page. In the beginning of the process the page shows him the way. Increasingly, however, the roles seem to become reversed. Then he takes the page by the hand and takes him to places where he would otherwise not come. Step by step he becomes master of his own will. When the virgin comes to the fore, said Steiner, it is a sign that wisdom is revealed to him, not through his own efforts but as a gift bestowed as grace.

Now the path leads into the depths, down many steps to an iron door with the following words in copper letters (copper is the metal of Venus): "Here lies buried Venus, that beauty which has undone many a great man both in fortune, honour, blessing and prosperity." When the alchemist has not built up a pure relation with these awesome powers of love, he is robbed. The alchemist who has gone through catharsis and does not "fall into the trap" of outer appearance, is able to withstand this trial.

As it says in the inscription on the door, Venus indeed lies buried here, but in the text it appears as if she is sleeping. First, Christian Rosenkreutz and the page arrive in a subterranean space and look upon "the most precious thing that nature ever created ... the king's treasury."

It is difficult to fully picture this triangular tomb. In the middle stands a copper kettle. In this kettle stands an angel carrying a strange tree in its arms. The fruits of this tree – and Christian Rosenkreutz does not immediately understand how this happens – fall into the kettle and melt, upon which they flow into three smaller kettles. Suddenly Christian Rosenkreutz speaks of this object not as a tomb but as an altar supported by three animals: an eagle, an ox and a lion. The fourth being belonging to it is the angel. We know these four beings from Ezekiel (1:5–10) and from the Book of Revelation (4:7) as the lion, the bull, the eagle and the human being. In the vision of Ezekiel it is apparent that these are not animals in the ordinary sense of the word, but lofty angel beings of the rank of the Cherubim. The text of Revelation also does not use the common word for animals (Greek *therion)* but *zoē,* living beings. Here, at the altar of the *Chymical Wedding*, the angel takes a special position in the midst of the three animals.

The page cannot help Christian Rosenkreutz with any further explanations; he can merely repeat what is written. He cannot help Christian Rosenkreutz understand the events, but he does know how the way continues through a copper door in the floor – that is, if he wants to go further. "I am still following you," says Christian Rosenkreutz. In the light of a torch kindled by the page they see Lady Venus. He dares not touch her. On a tablet behind her bed is written the inscription: "When the fruit of my tree shall be quite melted down then I shall awake and be the mother of a king."

A time will come when the power that is now still deeply sunk in the "sleep of Sleeping Beauty" will awaken. That will happen "when the fruit of my tree shall be quite melted down." Apparently that is not soon, for Christian Rosenkreutz has just seen the tree full of fruit. Creation produces, and reproduces, for millions of years. But in the dying existence of our earth we might imagine that this creative force will gradually decline and produce less and less "fruit," until one day the material part of the creation will have disappeared. This will happen at the stage that in the Book of Revelation is called the New Jerusalem, and in anthroposophy, Jupiter. Here, though, the words point to an even more distant future when the force that slumbers in creation will awaken, a time when a spiritual creation will exist. But that time, the time of Venus, is still far away.

When Christian Rosenkreutz and his page have mounted the stairs again, the latter shows the small flames burning in the four corners of the altar behind little doors. "From this heat the tree was forced continually to melt, yet it still produced new fruit." The "driving force" behind substance in this world is fire. The unusual expression used here is: a small taper of pyrites. The Greeks called this mineral *pyrites,* meaning fire-stone, flint. It is a stone that appears in sixty different crystalline forms in countless locations on the earth. It is evident that this mineral is connected with life because it can be found in many fossils (including shells and snails). Pyrites may form wherever organic material petrifies.

Again, the page is unable to answer his question as to the meaning of this. To the dismay of the two intruders, Lady Venus' factotum, Cupid, suddenly appears. Christian Rosenkreutz does not mention what he has seen. When Cupid has locked the copper door he marks Christian Rosenkreutz with a strange sign. "I cannot let it pass unrevenged," he says, and pricks the hand of the perpetrator with a hot arrowhead. This is the third time that Christian Rosenkreutz is injured. On the first day, in the dream of the tower, he is injured on his head by a stone. The chains there also injured both his feet so that he is lame. Just because he is injured he develops a certain vulnerability and receptivity, as becomes evident later in the day. "The more helpless we are, the more receptive to morality and religion we become," writes Novalis in his *Fragments.*

When Christian Rosenkreutz rejoins the group (called "the mercurialists"), Cupid laughs when he sees the drop of blood on his hand. He connects it with a time in which Christian Rosenkreutz will grow old, meaning in this case, that he will be rejuvenated. As it says in the alchemical text quoted earlier: "In no other manner than by his death can the human being be renewed and rejuvenated."

The virgin, still dressed in black velvet but with a laurel branch in her hand as a sign of victory, leads the group to a courtyard where a seemingly solemn scene is enacted. "In the court stood six coffins, and my companions thought nothing other than that the six Royal Persons lay in them, but I well observed the device." This is a theme we will hear more often. Empty sheaths apparently do not occur in the physical world alone, but also here, where we can be hoodwinked when we have seen a half-truth. In the solemn interment of the empty coffins we can already distinguish the portent of the resurrection: a banner (also in Christianity this is a symbol of the resurrection) showing the phoenix.

Subsequently they all travel to the place where the kings will be brought to life again: the Tower of Olympus. Mount Olympus was in Greek antiquity the home and seat of Zeus, whom the Romans called

Jupiter. It is of course not without foundation that in anthroposophy this name is used to indicate a future phase of creation. Just like the name Venus for an even later phase of creation, it originates from occult tradition.

When alchemists concerned themselves with "Jupiter," with the future of our creation, they had to brave the great sea of life forces (etheric forces) to find this future realm. In all ages there have been individuals who were able to read the future in the realm of spirit; they were called prophets and apocalyptics. We have a weak reflection of this in the word "foreshadowing," when something seems to foreshadow a future event. In the future, human beings will be more than just creatures; they will be co-creators. In the Book of Revelation, Christ announces this future condition with the words: "He who overcomes, I will grant him to sit on the throne with me, as I, too, have won the victory of the spirit and sit on the throne with my Father" (Rev.3:21 *M*). The throne here does not imply resting on one's laurels, but ruling, creating, ordering. The work that is awaiting Christian Rosenkreutz and his companions is about a creation in miniature: to "be helpful in restoring the present buried royal persons to life again."

Now seven ships sail across the sea in the formation of a pentagram with the mercurialists, the virgin and some crew members, and with the coffins secretly stowed on board. That we have to do here with a cosmic experience is shown in the imagery of the banners: they represent the five *Corpora Regularia* – an astronomical expression for Saturn, Mars, Earth, Venus, Mercury – and in the middle are the two ships with the banners of the Sun and the Moon. The planet Jupiter is missing, but that is where they are heading: the tower named Olympus. From the lake, the little ether world, they enter upon the great ether sea where one loses oneself if one does not travel in the sign of the pentagram. The pentagram is from olden times the sign of the human being and his form. Only those human beings who maintain the forces that belong to being human can preserve themselves in the space of the world of life. It is an endless ocean in which one otherwise loses one's footing.

The spiritual powers that inhabit the water – sea goddesses, nymphs and sirens – bring a gift that presages the future creation: a precious pearl. In the New Jerusalem the twelve gates are made of pearls. The imagery of Revelation indicates that the twelvefold access can only be found "by the pearls," the experience of bearing pain. At the same time, however, the lovely scene that follows also contains a temptation. Sirens form part of the airy party that accompanies the boat. In the trials which the Greek hero Odysseus has to go through, the illusionary world of the sirens is suggestively described. He can withstand this temptation only by stopping the ears of his companions with wax and ordering them to bind him tightly to the mast.

The hymn now sung by the nymphs contains in a certain sense all that lies at the foundation of creation. Goethe was so profoundly impressed by this poem that he worked it into a quintessence, which he dedicated to Charlotte von Stein:

> Whence are we born?
> From love.
> How would we be lost?
> Without love.
> What helps us overcome?
> Love.
> And can one find love?
> Through love.
> What lets us not be bored?
> Love.
> What will always unite us?
> Love.[4]

> *Woher sind wir geboren?*
> *Aus Lieb.*
> *Wie wären wir verloren?*
> *Ohn Lieb.*
> *Was hilft uns überwinden?*
> *Die Lieb.*
> *Kann man auch Liebe finden?*
> *Durch Lieb.*
> *Was lässt nicht langweilen?*
> *Die Lieb.*
> *Was soll uns stets vereinen?*
> *Die Lieb.*

All we are, all we have, we owe to this power. If the Godhead would for one single instant drop human beings from his love, they would cease to exist. Love is the power that can bring back together what has broken apart in creation. Here Venus is celebrated in her true and future essence!

In this heartwarming hymn a new bond is formed between the spiritual powers in nature (the world of life) and the human being. This bond is clearly symbolised when the nymphs receive a long red ribbon.

Christian Rosenkreutz also experiences this new bond with the powers of nature and the love that radiates from them. "I was at this time aware that Cupid began to work with me too, which yet tended by a very little towards my credit, and forasmuch as my giddiness is not likely to be beneficial to the reader, I am resolved to let it rest as it is. But this was the very wound that in the first book I received on the head in a dream." Enigmatic words. Apparently, he has become vulnerable, sensitive, by the wound he sustained, so that the temptation that emanates from these love forces is hard to overcome. Maybe an Odyssey in miniature?

They are received at the Tower of Olympus, which is built on a square island. The Greek philosopher Pythagoras taught that the creation was built on a square, the basis of the four elements. The tower has seven storeys, one for each phase of the alchemical process. "This tower was situated upon an island which was exactly square, and which was environed with a wall that was so firm and thick that I myself counted two hundred and sixty paces over." A number of commentators make the remark here that the number has to be 360. It is again the slow, plodding way we have seen before. "The tower itself was just as if seven round towers had been built one by another." In the descriptions of the sixth day we will become familiar with the tower, but then as seen from the inside: "the roof, which was wonderfully formed; for on the inside it was arched into seven hemispheres, of which the midmost was somewhat the highest, and had at the top a little round hole." The two descriptions agree precisely with each other.

It is an image of the ground of the physical world in the four elements: earth, water, air and fire; and on this ground the future creation is founded in seven phases. Again, the mercurialists are hoodwinked. Unknown to them, the coffins are brought into the tower. "Having come in this way to the gates of the tower, we were led a little aside by the wall, so that, as I well observed, the coffins might be brought into the tower without our taking notice; of this the rest knew nothing."

Then they are put to work and become collaborators in the sense of St Paul. The alchemists often based themselves on St Paul in their work. St Paul recognised that human beings who want to prepare themselves for the future must not just be God's creatures, but must also become God's fellow workers (1Cor.3:9).

The subsequent second stage in the series of seven alchemical processes is called sublimation. "The earthly impurity of all things must be eradicated by sublimation," the alchemist Arnaldus writes in his book *Rosarium Philosophorum*. This does not only take place in the chemical process we know as sublimation, but also in washing with water. The role played by human beings themselves is of key importance in these purification processes. Valentinus writes in *The Twelve Keys:* "... that all impure and blemished things are unworthy of our work ... Thus also our bodies must be swept and cleaned of all stains, so that in our birth perfection may prevail."

On the previous day the first stage, mortification, was enacted in a certain sense around them, outside of them. Now they have to provide all kinds of help and service, although the real work, the washing, is done by three virgins. In the subsequent stages on the sixth day the mercurialists become increasingly involved in the process.

At the end of this day, Christian Rosenkreutz is again a little step ahead of the other alchemists. "For my part I was not very much bothered about sleeping, and therefore walked out into the garden, and at length came as far as the wall; and because the heaven was at that time very clear, I could well drive away the time in contemplating the stars ... I found that this present night there would occur a conjunction of the planets, the like of which was not otherwise usually to be observed." The future creation is possible only in a marriage of heaven and earth.

Still, Christian Rosenkreutz experiences that he is at this stage not yet able to keep his footing out of his own forces in this unexplored territory: when the seven flames approach across the sea and a terrifying wind arises, he hurries back into the protection of the tower.

The Sixth Day

The Sixth Day

Next morning, after we had awakened one another, we sat together a while to discuss what might yet be the events to occur. For some were of the opinion that they should all be brought back to life again together. Others contradicted this, because the decease of the ancients was not only to restore life, but to increase it too to the young ones. Some imagined that they had not been put to death, but that others had been beheaded in their stead.

We now having talked together a pretty long while, in came the old man, and first saluting us, looked about him to see if all things were ready, and the processes sufficiently completed. We had so conducted ourselves as regards this that he had no fault to find with our diligence, so he placed all the glasses together, and put them into a case. Presently in came certain youths bringing with them some ladders, ropes, and large wings, which they laid down before us.

Then the old man began as follows: "My dear sons, each of you must this day constantly bear one of these three things about with him. Now you are free either to make a choice of one of them, or to cast lots about it."

We replied, "We would choose."

"No," he said, "let it rather go by lot."

Hereupon he made three little schedules. On one he wrote LADDER, on the second ROPE, on the third WINGS. These he put in a hat, and each man must draw, and whatever he got, that was to be his. Those who got the ropes imagined themselves to have the best of it, but I chanced to get a ladder, which afflicted me greatly, for it was twelve feet long, and pretty weighty, and I was forced to carry it, whereas the others could handsomely coil their ropes about them. And as for the wings, the old man joined them so closely onto the third group, as if they had grown upon them.

Hereupon he turned the cock, and then the fountain no longer ran, and we had to remove it from the middle out of the way. After all things were carried off, he took leave, taking with him the casket with the glasses, and locked the door fast after him, so that we imagined nothing other but that we had been imprisoned in this tower.

But it was hardly a quarter of an hour before a round hole at the very top was uncovered, where we saw our virgin, who called to us, and bade us good morrow, desiring us to come up. Those with the wings were instantly above and through the hole. Only those with the ropes were in an evil plight. For as soon as every one of us was up, he was commanded to draw up the ladder after him. At last each man's rope was hung on an iron hook, so everyone had to climb up by his rope as well as he could, which indeed was not accomplished without blisters.

Now as soon as we were all up, the hole was covered again, and we were kindly received by the virgin. This room was the whole breadth of the tower itself, having six very stately vestries raised a little above the room, and were entered by an ascent of three steps. In these vestries we were placed, there to pray for the life of the king and queen. Meanwhile the virgin went in and out of the little door A, till we were ready.

For as soon as our process was absolved, there was brought in by twelve persons (who were formerly our musicians), through the little door, and placed in the middle, a wonderful thing of longish shape, which my companions took only to be a fountain. But I well observed that the corpses lay in it, for the inner chest was of an oval figure, so large that six persons might well lie in it one by another. After which they again went forth, fetched their instruments, and conducted our virgin in, together with her female attendants, with a most delicate sound of music. The virgin carried a little casket, but the rest only branches and small lamps, and some lighted torches too. The torches were immediately given into our hands, and we were to stand about the fountain in this order.

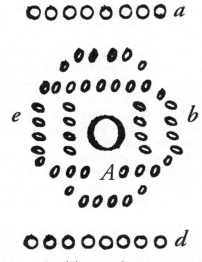

First stood the virgin at *A* with her attendants in a ring round about with the lamps and branches *c*. Next stood we with our torches *b*, then the musicians *a* in a long rank; last of all the rest of the virgins *d* in another long rank too. Now where the virgins came from, whether they lived in the castle, or whether they had been brought in by night, I do not know, for all their faces were covered with delicate white linen, so that I could not recognise any of them.

Hereupon the virgin opened the casket, in which there was a round thing wrapped up in a piece of green double taffeta. This she laid in the uppermost vessel, and then covered it with the lid, which was full of holes, and which had besides a rim through which she poured in some of the water which we had prepared the day before. Then the fountain began immediately to run, and to flow into the little vessel through four small pipes. Beneath the lower vessel there were many sharp points, on which the virgins stuck their lamps, so that the heat might reach the vessel, and make the water boil. Now the water beginning to simmer, it fell in upon the bodies by many little holes at *A*, and was so hot that it dissolved them all, and turned them into liquor. But what the above-mentioned round wrapped-up thing was, my companions did not know, but I understood that it was the Moor's head, from which the water drew so great a heat. At *b*, round about the great vessel, there were again many holes, in which they stuck their branches. Now whether this was done of necessity, or only for ceremony, I do not know. However, these branches were continually besprinkled by the fountain, and from them it afterwards dropped into the vessel something of a deeper yellow. This lasted for nearly two hours, the fountain still constantly running by itself; but the longer it ran, the fainter it was.

Meantime the musicians went their way, and we walked up and down in the room, and truly the room was made in such a way that we had opportunity enough to pass away our time. There were, for images, paintings, clockworks, organs, springing fountains, and the like, nothing forgotten.

Now it was near the time when the fountain ceased, and would run no longer, when the virgin commanded a round golden globe to be brought. But at the bottom of the fountain there was a tap, by which she let out all the matter that was dissolved by those hot drops (of which certain parts were then very red) into the globe. The rest of the water which remained above in the kettle was poured out. And so this fountain (which had now become much lighter) was again carried forth. Now whether it was opened elsewhere, or whether anything of the bodies that was further useful yet remained, I dare not say for certain. But this I know, that the water that was emptied into the globe was much heavier than six or even more of us were well able to bear, although going by its bulk it should have seemed not too heavy for one man. Now this globe having been got out of doors with much ado, we again sat alone, but I perceiving a trampling overhead, had an eye to my ladder.

Here one might take notice of the strange opinions my companions had concerning this fountain, for they, imagining that the bodies lay in the garden of the castle, did not know what to make of this kind of working, but I thanked God that I had awakened at so opportune a time, and that I had seen that which helped me the better in all the virgin's business.

After one quarter of an hour the cover above was again lifted off, and we were commanded to come up, which was done as before with wings, ladders and ropes. And it vexed me not a little that whereas the virgins could go up another way, we had to take so much toil; yet I could well judge that there must be some special reason for it, and we must leave something for the old man to do too. For even those with wings had no advantage by them other than when they had to climb through the hole.

Now we having got up there, and the hole having been shut again, I saw the globe hanging by a strong chain in the middle of the room. In this room was nothing but windows, and between two windows there was a door, which was covered with nothing other than a great polished looking-glass. And these windows and these looking-glasses were optically opposed to one another, so that although the sun (which was now shining exceedingly brightly) beat only upon one door, yet (after the windows towards the sun were opened, and the doors before the looking-glasses drawn aside) in all quarters of the room there were nothing but suns, which by artificial refractions beat upon the whole golden globe standing in the midst; and because (besides all this brightness) it was polished, it gave such a lustre, that none of us could open our eyes, but were forced to look out of the windows till the globe was well heated, and brought to the desired effect. Here I may well avow that in these mirrors I have seen the most wonderful spectacle that ever nature brought to light, for there were suns in all places, and the globe in the middle shone still brighter, so that we could no more endure it than the sun itself, except for one twinkling of an eye.

At length the virgin commanded the looking-glasses to be shut up again, and the windows to be made fast, and so to let the globe cool again a little; and this was done about seven o'clock. This we thought good, since we might now have a little leisure to refresh ourselves with breakfast. This treatment was again right philosophical, and we had no need to be afraid of intemperance, yet we had no want. And the hope of the future joy (with which the virgin continually comforted us) made us so jocund that we took no notice of any pains or inconvenience. And this I can truly say too concerning my companions of high quality, that their minds never ran after their kitchen or table, but their pleasure was only to attend upon this adventurous physic, and hence to contemplate the Creator's wisdom and omnipotency.

After we had taken our meal, we again settled down to work, for the globe, which with toil and labour we were to lift off the chain and set upon the floor, was sufficiently cooled. Now the dispute was how to get the globe in half, for we were commanded to divide it in the middle. The conclusion was that a sharp pointed diamond would best do it. Now when we had thus opened the globe, there was nothing more of redness to be seen, but a lovely great snow-white egg. It made us rejoice most greatly that this had been brought to pass so well. For the virgin was in perpetual care lest the shell might still be too tender. We stood round about this egg as jocund as if we ourselves had laid it. But the virgin made it be carried forth, and departed herself, too, from us again, and (as always) locked the door. But what she did outside with the egg, or whether it were in some way privately handled, I do not know, neither do I believe it. Yet we were again to wait together for a quarter of an hour, till the third hole was opened, and we by means of our instruments came to the fourth stone or floor.

In this room we found a great copper vessel filled with yellow sand, which was warmed by a gentle fire. Afterwards the egg was raked up in it, that it might therein come to perfect maturity. This vessel was exactly square; upon one side stood these two verses, written in great letters.

O. BLI. TO. BIT. MI. LI.

KANT. I. VOLT. BIT. TO. GOLT.*

On the second side were these three words:

SANITAS. NIX. HASTA. (Health, Snow, Lance.)

The third had only one word:

F.I.A.T.

But on the reverse was an entire inscription running thus:

QUOD.

IGNIS: AER: AQUA: TERRA:

SANCTIS REGUM ET REGINARUM NOSTR:

CINERIBUS.

ERIPERE NON POTUERUNT

FIDELIS CHYMICORUM TURBA

IN HANC URNAM

CONTULIT.

ANNO 1459.

* Unknown meaning.

What
Fire: Air: Water: Earth
Were unable to rob
From the holy ashes
Of our kings and queens
Was gathered by the faithful flock
Of alchemists
In this urn
A.D. 1459.

Now whether the the egg were hereby meant, I leave to the learned to dispute; yet I do my part, and omit nothing undeclared. Our egg being now ready was taken out, but it needed no cracking, for the bird that was in it soon freed himself, and showed himself very jocund, yet he looked very bloody and unshapen. We first set him upon the warm sand, so the virgin commanded that before we gave him anything to eat, we should be sure to make him fast, otherwise he would give us all work enough. This being done too, food was brought him, which surely was nothing else than the blood of the beheaded, diluted again with prepared water; by which the bird grew so fast under our eyes, that we saw well why the virgin gave us such warning about him. He bit and scratched so devilishly about him, that could he have had his will upon any of us, he would have despatched him. Now he was wholly black, and wild, so other food was brought him, perhaps the blood of another of the royal persons; whereupon all his black feathers moulted again, and instead of them there grew out snow-white feathers. He was somewhat tamer too, and more docile. Nevertheless we did not yet trust him. At the third feeding his feathers began to be so curiously coloured that in all my life I never saw such beautiful colours. He was also exceedingly tame, and behaved himself in such friendly manner with us, that (the virgin consenting) we released him from his captivity.

Our virgin began: "Since by your diligence, and our old man's consent, the bird has attained both his life and the highest perfection, this is a good reason that he should also be joyfully consecrated by us."

Herewith she commanded that dinner should be brought, and that we should again refresh ourselves, since the most troublesome part of our work was now over, and it was fitting that we should begin to enjoy our past labours. We began to make ourselves merry together. However, we still had all our mourning clothes on, which seemed somewhat reproachful to our mirth. Now the virgin was perpetually inquisitive, perhaps to find to which of us her future purpose might prove serviceable. But her discourse was for the most part about smelting; and it pleased her well when one seemed expert in such compendious manuals as do particularly commend an artist. This dinner lasted not more than three quarters of an hour, which we still for the most part spent with our bird, and we had to constantly feed him with his food, but he still remained much the same size. After dinner we were not allowed long to digest our food, before the virgin, together with the bird, departed from us.

The fifth room was set open to us, where we went as before, and offered our services. In this room a bath was prepared for our bird, which was so coloured with a fine white powder that it had the appearance of milk. Now it was at first cool when the bird was set into it. He was mighty well pleased with it, drinking of it, and pleasantly sporting in it. But after it began to heat because of the lamps that were placed under it, we had enough to do to keep him in the bath. We therefore clapped a cover on the vessel, and allowed him to thrust his head out through a hole, till he had in this way lost all his feathers in the bath, and was as smooth as a new-born child; yet the heat did him no further harm, at which I much marvelled, for the feathers were completely consumed in this bath, and the bath was thereby tinged blue.

At length we gave the bird air, and he sprang out of the vessel of his own accord, and he was so glittering and smooth that it was a pleasure to behold. But because he was still somewhat wild, we had to put a collar with a chain about his neck, and so led him up and down the room. Meanwhile a strong fire was made under the vessel, and the bath boiled away till it all came down to a blue stone, which we took out, and having first pounded it, ground it with a stone, and finally with this colour began to paint the bird's skin all over. Now he looked much more strange, for he was all blue, except the head, which remained white.

Herewith our work on this storey was performed, and we (after the virgin with her blue bird was departed from us) were called up through the hole to the sixth storey, where we were greatly troubled. For in the middle was placed a little altar, in every way like that in the king's hall above described. Upon this stood the six aforementioned particulars, and he himself (the bird) made the seventh.

First of all the little fountain was set before him, out of which he drunk a good draught. Afterwards he pecked the white serpent until she bled a great deal. This blood we had to receive into a golden cup, and pour it down the bird's throat, who was greatly averse to it. Then we dipped the serpent's head in the fountain, upon which she revived again, and crept into her death's-head, so that I saw her no more for a long time after. Meantime the sphere turned constantly, until it made the desired conjunction. Immediately the clock struck one, upon which another conjunction was set going. Then the clock struck two. Finally, while we were observing the third conjunction, and this was indicated by the clock, the poor bird submissively laid down his neck upon the book of his own accord, and willingly allowed his head to be smitten off (by one of us chosen for this by lot). However, he yielded not a drop of blood until his breast was opened, and then the blood spurted out so fresh and clear as if it had been a fountain of rubies. His death went to our hearts, and yet we could well judge that a naked bird would stand us in little stead. So we let it be, and moved the little altar away and assisted the virgin to burn the body to ashes (together with the little tablet hanging by) with fire kindled by the little taper; and afterwards to cleanse the same several times, and to lay them in a box of cypress wood.

Here I cannot conceal what a trick was played on myself and three others. After we had thus diligently taken up the ashes, the virgin began to speak as follows:

"My lords, here we are in the sixth room, and we have only one more before us, in which our trouble will be at an end, and then we shall return home again to our castle, to awaken our most gracious lords and ladies. Now I could heartily wish that all of you, as you are here together, had behaved yourselves in such a way that I might have commended to our most renowned king and queen, and you might have obtained a suitable reward; yet contrary to my desire, I have found amongst you these four lazy and sluggish workers (herewith she pointed at me and three others). Yet, according to my goodwill to each and every one, I am not willing to deliver them up to deserved punishment. However, so that such negligence may not remain wholly unpunished, I am resolved thus concerning them, that they shall only be excluded from the future seventh and most glorious action of all the rest, and so they shall incur no further blame from their royal majesties."

In what a state we now were at this speech I leave others to consider. For the virgin knew so well how to keep her countenance, that the water soon ran over our baskets, and we esteemed ourselves the most unhappy of all men. After this the virgin caused one of her maids (of whom there were many always at hand) to fetch the musicians, who were to blow us out of doors with cornets, with such scorn and derision that they themselves could hardly blow for laughing. But it afflicted us particularly greatly that the virgin so vehemently laughed at our weeping, anger and impatience, and that there might well perhaps be some amongst our companions who were glad of this misfortune of ours.

But it proved otherwise, for as soon as we had come out of the door, the musicians told us to be of good cheer and follow them up the winding stairs. They led us past the seventh floor to under the roof, where we found the old man, whom we had not hitherto seen, standing upon a little round furnace. He received us in a friendly manner, and heartily congratulated us that we had been chosen for this by the virgin; but after he understood the fright we had received, his belly was ready to burst with laughing that we had taken such good fortune so badly.

"Hence," said he, "my dear sons, learn that man never knows how well God intended him."

During this discourse the virgin also came running in with her little box, and (after she had laughed at us enough) emptied her ashes into another vessel, and filled hers again with other stuff, saying she must now go and cast a mist before the other artists' eyes, and that we in the meantime should obey the old lord in whatsoever he commanded us, and not remit our former diligence. Herewith she departed from us into the seventh room into which she called our companions. Now what she did first with them there, I cannot tell, for not only were they most earnestly forbidden to speak of it, but we also, because of our work, did not dare peep on them through the ceiling.

But this was our work. We had to moisten the ashes with our previously prepared water until they became altogether like a very thin dough, after which we set the matter over the fire, till it was well heated. Then we cast it, hot like this, into two little forms or moulds, and let it cool a little.

Here we had leisure to look a while at our companions through certain crevices made in the floor. They were now very busy at a furnace, and each had to blow up the fire himself with a pipe, and they stood blowing about it like this, as if they were wondrously preferred before us in this. And this blowing lasted until our old man roused us to our work again, so that I cannot say what was done afterwards.

We opened our little forms, and there appeared two beautiful, bright and almost transparent little images, the like of which man's eye never saw, a male and a female, each of them only four inches long, and what surprised us most greatly was that they were not hard, but lithe and fleshy, like other human bodies, yet they had no life; so that I most assuredly believe that the Lady Venus's image was also made after some such manner.

These angelically fair babes we first laid upon two little satin cushions, and looked at them for a good while, till we were almost besotted by such exquisite objects. The old lord warned us to forbear, and continually to instil the blood of the bird (which had been received into a little golden cup) drop after drop into the mouths of the little images, from which they appeared to increase; and whereas they were before very small, they were now (according to proportion) much more beautiful, so that all painters ought to have been here, and would have been ashamed of their art in respect of these productions of nature. Now they began to grow so big that we lifted them from the little cushions, and had to lay them upon a long table, which was covered with white velvet. The old man also commanded us to cover them over up to the breast with a piece of the fine white double taffeta, which, because of their unspeakable beauty, almost went against us. But to be brief, before we had quite used up the blood in this way, they were already in their perfect full growth. They had golden-yellow, curly hair, and the above-mentioned figure of Venus was nothing to them.

But there was not yet any natural warmth or sensibility in them. They were dead figures, yet of a lively and natural colour; and since care was to be taken that they did not grow too big, the old man would not permit anything more to be given to them, but covered their faces too with the silk, and caused the table to be stuck round about with torches. Here I must warn the reader not to imagine these lights to have been put there out of necessity, for the old man's intent hereby was only that we should not observe when the soul entered into them; and indeed we should not have noticed it, had I not twice before seen the flames. However, I permitted the other three to remain with their own belief, neither did the old man know that I had seen anything more. Hereupon he asked us to sit down on a bench over against the table.

Presently the virgin came in too, with the music and all necessities, and carried two curious white garments, the like of which I had never seen in the castle, nor can I describe them, for I thought that they were nothing other than crystal; but they were soft, and not transparent; so that I cannot describe them. These she laid down on a table, and after she had disposed her virgins upon a bench round about, she and the old man began many slight-of-hand tricks about the table, which was done only to blind us. This (as I told you) was managed under the roof, which was wonderfully formed; for on the inside it was arched into seven hemispheres, of which the midmost was somewhat the highest, and had at the top a little round hole, which was nevertheless shut, and was observed by no-one else.

After many ceremonies six virgins came in, each of whom carried a large trumpet, around which were rolled a green, glittering and burning material like a wreath. The old man took one of these, and after he had removed some of the lights at the top of the table, and uncovered their faces, he placed one of the trumpets upon the mouth of one of the bodies in such a way that the upper and wider end of it was directed just towards the aforementioned hole. Here my companions always looked at the images, but I had other thoughts, for as soon as the foliage or wreath about the shank of the trumpet was kindled, I saw the hole at the top open, and a bright stream of fire shooting down the tube, and passing into the body; whereupon the hole was covered again, and the trumpet removed. With this device my companions were deluded, so that they imagined that life came into the image by means of the fire of the foliage, for as soon as he received the soul his eyes twinkled, although he hardly stirred. The second time he placed another tube upon its mouth, and kindled it again, and the soul was let down through the tube. This as repeated for each of them three times, after which all the lights were extinguished and carried away. The velvet coverings of the table were cast over them, and immediately a birthing bed was unlocked and made ready, into which, thus wrapped up, they were born. And after the coverings were taken off them, they were neatly laid by each other, and with the curtains drawn before them, they slept a good while.

Now it was also time for the virgin to see how other artists behaved themselves. They were well pleased because, as the virgin afterwards informed me, they were to work in gold, which is indeed a piece of this art, but not the most principal, most necessary, and best. They had indeed too a part of these ashes, so that they imagined nothing other than that the whole bird was provided for the sake of gold, and that life must thereby be restored to the deceased.

Meantime we sat very still, waiting for our married couple to awake. About half an hour was spent like this. Then the wanton Cupid presented himself again, and after he had saluted us all, flew to them behind the curtain, tormenting them until they awakened. This was a cause of great amazement to them, for they imagined that they had slept from the very hour in which they were beheaded until now. Cupid, after he had awakened them, and renewed their acquaintance with one another, stepped aside a little, and allowed them both to get themselves together a bit better, meantime playing his tricks with us; and at length he wanted to have the music brought in, to be somewhat merrier.

Not long after, the virgin herself came in, and after she had most humbly saluted the young king and queen (who found themselves rather faint) and kissed their hands, she brought them the two aforementioned strange garments, which they put on, and so stepped forth. Now there were already prepared two very strange chairs, in which they placed themselves. And they were congratulated with most profound reverence by us, for which the king himself most graciously returned his thanks, and again reassured us of all grace.

It was already about five o'clock, so they could no longer stay, but as soon as the best of their furniture could be laden, we had to attend the young royal persons down the winding stairs, through all doors and watches to the ship. In this they embarked, together with certain virgins and Cupid, and sailed so very swiftly that we soon lost sight of them; but they were met (as I was informed) by certain stately ships. Thus in four hours' time they had gone many leagues out to sea. After five o'clock the musicians were charged to carry all things back again to the ships, and to make themselves ready for the voyage. But because this took rather a long time, the old lord commanded a party of his concealed soldiers to come out. They had hitherto been planted in a wall, so that we had not noticed any of them, whereby I observed that this tower was well provided against opposition. Now these soldiers made quick work with our stuff, so that nothing more remained to be done but to go to supper.

The table being completely furnished, the virgin brought us again to our companions, where we were to carry ourselves as if we had truly been in a lamentable condition, and forbear laughing. But they were always smiling to one another, although some of them sympathised with us too. At this supper the old lord was also with us, who was a most sharp inspector over us; for no-one could propound anything so discreetly, but he knew either how to confute it, or to amend it, or at least to give some good information on it. I learned a great deal from this lord, and it would be very good if each one would apply themselves to him, and take notice of his procedure, for then things would not miscarry so often and so unfortunately.

After we had taken our nocturnal refreshment, the old lord took us into his closets of rarities, which were dispersed here and there amongst the bulwarks; where we saw such wonderful productions of nature, and other things too which man's wit, in imitation of nature, had invented, that we needed another year to survey them sufficiently. Thus we spent a good part of the night by candlelight. At last, because we were more inclined to sleep than to see many rarities, we were lodged in rooms in the wall, where we had not only costly and good beds, but also extraordinarily handsome chambers, which made us wonder all the more why we were forced to undergo so many hardships the day before. In this chamber I had good rest, and being for the most part without care, and weary with continual labour, the gentle rushing of the sea helped me to a sound and sweet sleep, for I continued in one dream from eleven o'clock till eight in the morning.

The Sixth Day: Commentary

The alchemists describe the development from the primal beginnings to the goal of creation – from *prima materia,* first matter, to *materia ultima,* ultimate matter – as the way from virgin to bride. The primal beginning of matter is virginal. The way ends in communion, union of two worlds which for eons went, in part, their own ways. "He who brings a thing into the state to which it was ordained and destined by nature is a true alchemist," wrote Paracelsus.

On the sixth day the path of development leads for the first time consistently upward, in seven stages. Earlier, the path led into the depths (Venus) or into the widths of space (the voyage). Besides the virgin, there is now at certain times another guide – the one who had received them the previous day, the ancient man, the warden of the tower. At the end of this day he proves to possess great life wisdom. "I learned a great deal from this lord, and it would be very good if each one would apply themselves to him, and take notice of his procedure, for then things would not miscarry so often and so unfortunately." Just as a young man expresses pure willpower, in the old – as we can observe in life around us – life experience bestows wisdom.

For a moment it seems as if the mercurialists are allowed to choose by what means they wish to ascend: ladders, ropes or wings. The old man said:

> "You are free either to make a choice of one of them, or to cast lots about it."
> We replied, "We would choose."
> "No," he said, "let it rather go by lot."

Is that life wisdom? At first sight it rather looks like an imposition of authority. Maybe it is a test: Have you come to the point in your development that everything you encounter can also become your own will? Can you leave everything to destiny, not as a fatalist or fanatic, but as a human being who complies with heart and soul – as in "Just say yes to life!" Novalis put it in the enigmatic words: "All that happens is my will." It takes a lot in the maelstrom of daily life, in all the heights and depths of life, to be able to say: All that happens,

I have willed. There are people who understandably rebel when they hear these words.

There are three different ways to ascend in the tower. With wings it is easy and quick. With ropes it takes great effort and blisters. In between is the third way, the ladder on which one goes up step by step. This is naturally the way of Christian Rosenkreutz. We have seen it before. But there is one great difference with the first time he ascended. In the dream of the first day he had to hold on to the rope and was pulled up. Now he is no longer pulled up; he has to rise by his own forces. When we compare such moments in the *Chymical Wedding* with each other, we discover that he has made progress on his way.

Before the real alchemical work begins, the mercurialists offer prayers for the life of the king and queen. Then a heavy rectangular object is carried in by twelve men. Christian Rosenkreutz is the only one who understands what it is. While the others think it is a fountain, he recognises by the form that the three royal couples must be hidden in it. To the very end of the path of initiation he is able to observe with different eyes than the other alchemists, who experience spiritual reality only in part.

The virgin then brings in a little chest that is to play a very important part in the alchemical process. In it is the Moor's head, which is placed in a strange kind of vessel with a lid full of holes. Under the vessel stands the heavy object in which the six bodies are lying. This object is placed in a great kettle with a lid full of holes. The chest with the Moor's head is placed on top in a smaller kettle which also has a lid full of holes. Maidens now appear, led by Lady Alchimia. They stick branches into the holes of the lid of the lower kettle. Finally, the water that the mercurialists had prepared the previous day is poured into the two kettles, and the maidens place lights under the lower kettle. When the water is thus heated a double fountain starts working: from the Moor's head to the branches, and from the branches to the six bodies in the lower kettle. There are, therefore, three different realms: at the bottom the beheaded bodies; in the middle the branches that change the colour of the water; and at the top the Moor's head. "I understood that it was the Moor's head, from which the water drew so great a heat."

The Moor is the "hothead," who did the "dirty work," the killing of the three royal couples.

It looks like the world turned upside down: this lowest, darkest part of the human being represented by the Moor is placed on top and is in a certain sense the driving force. The lower ego, the domain of desire, receives a decisive role here. (An eloquent expression of this crucial element is shown in Figure 8.) The unique aspect of the Rosicrucians and alchemists is that they give the lower ego an important place. They do not, like some movements in mysticism and several strict Christian churches, want to stifle the ego.

This brings me back to the theme of the double that comes to the fore again at the end of the *Chymical Wedding* (the porter or guardian at the gate). Our double – Jung also calls it our shadow – has everything to do with the ego and its qualities. All the egoistic, negative characteristics a person has, acknowledged or not, are in a certain sense nourishment for the double. They give him the chance to make himself great so that, in the end, you sometimes can no longer recognise the human being behind the double. Just as the Rosicrucians handle the earth with respect, they also treat this lowest part of the human being with respect. For it is precious "raw material." As ore can be smelted into metals, so can this raw material be transformed into the most noble nature in the human being, from a temptation into a force.

In the meantime we have arrived at the third phase of the alchemical process.

1. *Mortificatio* – the death of the Royal Pairs
2. *Sublimatio* – washing the bodies
3. *Dissolutio* – dissolution

The dissolution process is quite literally described here: "the water beginning to simmer, it fell in upon the bodies by many little holes ... and was so hot that it dissolved them all, and turned them into liquor."

These three stages are often called the little work in alchemy. They bring the old creation to an endpoint. By death, washing and dissolution, matter is brought back to its pure state as much as possible.

EMBLEMA **XLV.** *De secretis Naturæ.* **189**
Sol & ejus umbra perficiunt opus.

EPIGRAMMA XLV.

SOL, *fax clara poli, non corpora densa penétrat,*
 Hinc illi adverss partibus umbra manet :
Vilior hæc rebus quamvis est omnibus, usu
 Attamen Astronomis commoda multa tulit :
Plura Sophis sed dona dedit SOL, *ejus & umbra,*
 Aurifera quoniam perficit artis opus.

Figure 8. Illustration from Michael Maier, Atalanta Fugiens, *Oppenheim 1617.*

4. The fourth phase of the alchemical process has a mediating
   function between the little work and the great work, between
   origin and goal. It forms the transition to the rebirth. In the
   Chymical Wedding this middle phase is described in great
   detail.

For the sake of completeness I will briefly mention here the three
phases of the great work that now follow. In his book *Alchemy,* Titus
Burckhardt sums it up as follows: "The first three phases indicate
the spiritualisation of the body; the last three the embodiment of the
spirit, or solidification of the volatile – *solve et coagula* (dissolve and
solidify).

5. *Coagulatio* – coagulation of the volatile – is the name of the
   fifth phase in the process: the images of the little boy and
   girl that come forth from the fire.
6. *Animatio* – ensoulment of the royal couple – with the six
   trumpets.
7. *Glorificatio* – celebration of the royal couple – awakening,
   clothing, thrones.[1]

Let us go back to the fourth phase which in the *Chymical Wedding*
encompasses a range of transformations. On the third storey,* a
golden sphere, containing the red liquid of the phase of dissolution,
is hanging from the ceiling in the middle of the room. By means
of mirrors placed all around, the light of the sun is multiplied and
directed onto the polished sphere.

In all quarters of the room there were nothing but suns, which
by artificial refractions beat upon the whole golden globe
standing in the midst; and because (besides all this brightness)
it was polished, it gave such a lustre, that none of us could
open our eyes.

It is as if the promise of the first token is fulfilled here: *Deus Lux
Solis* (see the First Day).

* The text mentions seven storeys; the ground floor is the first one.

From the heated sphere a snow-white egg emerges. Not only is the egg a familiar symbol of the Resurrection, for the alchemists it was also the emblem of union: "The egg of a bird that has in itself both seeds, of man and woman."[2] This is the moment in the fourth phase that in alchemy is called animatio: awakening the deceased to life. The fact that the alchemist is fully involved in this process can be recognised in the playful words: "We stood round about this egg as jocund as if we ourselves had laid it."

This may be a good place to consider the colours. The alchemists recognised seven colours between white and black that played a role in the chymical process. Black was the colour of the first phase. Subsequently, the process went through a number of the colours of the rainbow, but also through white, and then through the "tail of the peacock," all colours simultaneously. Finally, the Philosopher's Stone was described as red. We could compare this course through all the colours with a musical scale beginning with the key-note and ending in the octave. In this image then, the alchemists searched for the octave of the material world.

On the fourth floor, the workers find a cryptic text. *Fiat,* "may it become," is perhaps its key word. Do not accept the world as it is, but bring the creation to perfection. Where nature ends, that is where alchemy begins. The inscription on the kettle with the egg reads:

> What
> Fire: Air: Water: Earth
> Were unable to rob
> From the holy ashes
> Of our kings and queens
> Was gathered by the faithful flock
> Of alchemists
> In this urn [the egg].
> A.D. 1459.

The year 1459 is the year in which the *Chymical Wedding* takes place; this same year is printed on the original title page.

The creature that emerges from the egg is an awkward, clumsy product of the new creation. In a certain sense all the troubles are starting from the beginning again. "He bit and scratched so devilishly about him, that could he have had his will upon any of us, he would have despatched him. Now he was wholly black, and wild." The alchemists called this stage the dragon. Next, it becomes white, the stage of the swan. Then it changes to all the colours of the rainbow: "so curiously coloured that in all my life I never saw such beautiful colours." As was mentioned above, this is the stage of the tail of the peacock belonging to Venus. The more the bird is fed, the tamer it becomes. When things are quiet again, the virgin begins to ask questions. "Her discourse was for the most part about smelting; and it pleased her well when one seemed expert in such compendious manuals as do particularly commend an artist."

On the fifth floor there is a jovial mood in the room. It is somewhat like the splashing of a child in a bathtub. "Now it was at first cool when the bird was set into it. He was mighty well pleased with it, drinking of it, and pleasantly sporting in it. But after it began to heat because of the lamps that were placed under it, we had enough to do to keep him in the bath." Hardly has the bird lost all its feathers, colouring the water blue, when what was dissolved has to be made hard again: the water is evaporated until all that remains is a blue stone. "The entire process of the philosophical work is nothing other than dissolving and hardening again; namely dissolving the body and hardening the spirit." (Jean d'Espagnet, *Arcanum Hermeticae philosophiae,* 1623).

The blue stone is crushed to powder and the bird is painted with it. Rudolf Steiner called the colour blue "lustre of the soul." We have left the realm of death and beginning life (the egg) behind us, and are approaching the realm of the soul.

Initiation into the secrets of the earth is a path of unremitting sacrifice. This is shown again when on the next floor, the sixth, the bird is killed on an altar. The six attributes of the "bloody wedding" on the fourth day are used again. This phase, in which the bird willingly lets itself be killed, is called the stage of the pelican in alchemy. "He yielded not a drop of blood until his breast was opened, and then the blood spurted out so fresh and clear as if it had been a fountain of rubies." In olden times it was imagined that the red spot on the breast of a pelican was its own heart's blood with which the bird fed its young.

Finally, the dead bird has to arise like a phoenix from its ashes: it is reborn in the form of the two images of a little boy and girl. The entire process encompassing this middle phase between the little work and the great work consists of animals: dragon – swan – peacock – pelican – and finally phoenix. But before the phoenix stage the bird is burnt to ashes. The alchemists attributed precious properties to ash, indispensable in the process. One might call it the first building block for the new creation. One of the later offshoots of the Rosicrucian movement says of ash: *in cinere germinante terram novam* (in ash the new earth germinates).[3]

Where matter comes to an endpoint, loses all structure and turns into chaos, that is where some aspect of the future creation is able to connect with this matter. The traditional text of a Protestant burial ritual says it in the words: "Earth to earth, ashes to ashes, dust to dust, in the hope of eternal life." In such rituals we can still find traces of this ancient wisdom; though in our time we hardly have any understanding of the actual meaning of such words. Ashes, then, are the germ of a new creation.

Again, we can note a marked difference between what went before and the current stage. At the death of the royal couples Christian Rosenkreutz had only to watch. Now one of the alchemists, chosen by lot, has to kill the bird. They become co-executors of a creation that sometimes expresses itself in destruction.

In an unexpected turn of events, the virgin sets four of the mercurialists apart, including Christian Rosenkreutz, and excludes them from the "crown on the work," the conclusion of the great work on the seventh floor. "In what a state we now were at this speech I leave others to consider. For the virgin knew so well how to keep her countenance, that the water soon ran over our baskets, and we esteemed ourselves the most unhappy of all men ... But it proved otherwise, for as soon as we had come out of the door, the musicians told us to be of good cheer and follow them up the winding stairs. They led us past the seventh floor to under the roof." As it turns out, there is an eighth floor, which had not been noticed before. Together with a small group of initiates, Christian Rosenkreutz goes through an even higher phase of development than is known to most alchemists.

On this eighth floor he literally has an overview. However, he does not receive this opportunity until he has lost the remainder of his self-consciousness. The word *burgher* is derived from the word *burg* (castle or stronghold) via *burgh* (borough). We owe our daily, ordinary consciousness of self in part to the transition of the Middle Ages to modern times, when burghers could feel themselves free within the walls of their cities. Presently, we have the *burg* of our closed personalities in which we dwell safely and soundly. This is the form of consciousness of self that the four chosen ones have to lose. To this end, the virgin uses a radical device: humiliation and mockery. "But after he [the old man] understood the fright we had received, his belly was ready to burst with laughing that we had taken such good fortune so badly. 'Hence,' said he, 'my dear sons, learn that man never knows how well God intended him'." That is life wisdom that is most opportune for us also.

Only at this point is the great middle stage of the sevenfold alchemical process completed, and now begins the making of the "paste" in the fifth phase, called *coagulatio,* precipitation, coagulation. The ash is mixed with previously prepared water. When after the resulting paste is heated and formed the moulds are opened, they contain two little human forms. "...they were not hard, but lithe and fleshy, like other human bodies, yet they had no life; so that I most assuredly believe that the Lady Venus's image was also made after some such manner" – namely through love.

At this point the initiates almost come to a stop on their path of development. "We ... looked at them for a good while, till we were almost besotted by such exquisite objects. The old lord warned us to forbear ..." The venture remains a risky one, for nothing is so dangerous as thinking you have made it before you have reached the end.

The six royal persons have become two; the soul forces, which go their own separate ways in the spiritual world, have in this higher stage become a unity of two, the future king and queen. However, they do not receive these titles until the very last stage; at this point they are still images of children. They are covered with white silk. The virgin lays clothes on a table in which they are not yet dressed. "[She] carried two curious white garments, the like of which I had never seen in the castle, nor can I describe them, for I thought that they were nothing other than crystal; but they were soft, and not transparent; so that I cannot describe them." Here we have a description of the indestructible "garment" of life forces, which Christian Rosenkreutz receives in the initiation. At all times, the "white garment" has been the expression of the pure life body or ether body. Rudolf Steiner says of the great initiate Christian Rosenkreutz that he has an indestructible ether body; this means that he is at all times, living on earth or not, able to create connections with his fellow human beings on earth. A number of great initiates are known to be "present," and able to make themselves known on earth, under all circumstances.

Once more, Christian Rosenkreutz is the only one who sees what takes place in this sixth stage. It is the stage of ensoulment. Up to this point the images have been lifeless. The "life sheath" is lying beside them. The new creation has yet to be awakened to life. The only one who observes this is Christian Rosenkreutz. He notices that there is a small round hole in the dome of this eighth floor. Six maidens appear with six trumpets. One trumpet is put to the lips of one of the images so that it looks as if it is being blown. A flammable material has been wound around the bell of the trumpet, which is directed toward the opening in the ceiling. "...as soon as the foliage or wreath about the shank of the trumpet was kindled, I saw the hole at the top open, and a bright stream of fire shooting down the tube, and passing into the body." Christian Rosenkreutz sees that what is taking place up there is a re-creation, a new inspiration *(in-spiro* is blowing in). A spiritual being breathes life into the new human being. Thus the first Adam was created by the life-breath of God; now it is the new Adam, the second Adam as St Paul also calls him, who is born. For each of the two images this inspiration occurs three times; one could imagine once for the life body, once for the soul and once for the spirit.

At this point the two persons are left to sleep for a time. The only thing that is still lacking when they awaken is human love. In the seventh stage, which now follows, Cupid sets the crown on the work; he awakens them and sees to it that they recognise each other. It is not yet time for mercurial activity between the couple; Cupid too has to let the newly created beings come to themselves. In the words of the 1613 alchemical work *Turba Philosophorum:* "When the soul has been poured into the body, a crowned king arises."

They are dressed in colourful clothes – after the garment of life forces they receive the sheath of the human soul – and embark on a waiting vessel. After they have left for the continent, soldiers put all their possessions on board the remaining ships. Only now does

Christian Rosenkreutz notice that the tower is closely guarded. Why is that needed? The new creation is taboo for unauthorised persons. Whoever does not have the "nature of the virgin" cannot enter here.

Now the two groups, which had been separated on the seventh and eighth floors, come together again. The four quietly endure the mockery of those who had stayed behind; the latter had worked with gold. Here this does not mean they had been engaged in false alchemy. They were long past that phase: "they were to work in gold, which is indeed a piece of this art, but not the most principal, most necessary, and best," says Christian Rosenkreutz of their work.

After the old man has shared his wisdom with them and has shown them creations of nature and alchemy ("things ... which man's wit, in imitation of nature, had invented") they go to bed. And finally, for once in those seven days, Christian Rosenkreutz has a carefree night's sleep.

The Seventh Day

The Seventh Day

After eight o'clock I woke up, and quickly made myself ready, wanting to return again into the tower; but the dark passages in the wall were so many and various, that I wandered a good while before I could find the way out. The same happened to the rest too, till at last we all met again in the nethermost vault, and entirely yellow apparel was given to us, together with our golden fleeces. At this time the virgin declared to us that we were Knights of the Golden Stone, of which we were before ignorant.

After we had made ourselves ready, and taken our breakfast, the old man presented each of us with a medal of gold.

On one side were these words:

AR. NAT. MI.

(Art is the Priestess of Nature)

On the other these:

TEM. NA. F.

(Nature is the Daughter of Time.)

He exhorted us moreover that we should try to take nothing more than this token of remembrance. Herewith we went forth to the sea, where our ships lay, so richly equipped that it was not possible but that such amazing things must first have been brought there. The ships were twelve in number, six of ours, and six of the old lord's, who caused his ships to be freighted with well appointed soldiers. But he himself came to us in our ship, where we were all together. In the first the musicians, of which the old lord also had a great number, seated themselves; they sailed before us to shorten the time. Our flags were the twelve celestial signs, and we sat in Libra. Besides other things our ship also had a noble and curious clock, which showed us all the minutes. The sea was so calm, too, that it was a singular pleasure to sail. But what surpassed all the rest was the old man's discourse; he knew so well how to pass away our time with wonderful stories, that I could have been content to sail with him all my life long.

Meanwhile the ships passed on in haste, for before we had sailed two hours the mariner told us that he already saw the whole lake almost covered with ships, by which we could conjecture that they had come out to meet us, which proved true. For as soon as we had come out of the sea into the lake by the aforementioned river, there before us were five hundred ships, one of which sparkled with gold and precious stones, and in which sat the king and queen, together with other lords, ladies, and virgins of high birth. As soon as they were well in sight of us the pieces were discharged on both sides, and there was such a din of trumpets, shawms, and kettle-drums that all the ships upon the sea capered again. Finally, as soon as we came near they brought our ships together, and so made a stand.

Immediately the old Atlas stepped forth on the king's behalf, making a short but handsome oration, in which he welcomed us, and asked whether the royal presents were ready. The rest of my companions were in great amazement, where this king should come from, for they imagined nothing other than that they would have to awaken him again. We allowed them to continue in their amazement, and acted as if it seemed strange to us too. After Atlas' oration out stepped our old man, making a rather longer reply, in which he wished the king and queen all happiness and increase, after which he delivered up a curious small casket. What was in it, I do not know, but it was committed to Cupid to keep, who hovered between the king and queen.

After the oration was finished, they again let off a joyful volley of shot, and so we sailed on a good time together, till at length we arrived at another shore. This was near the first gate at which I first entered. At this place again there attended a great multitude of the king's family together with some hundreds of horses. Now as soon as we came to shore, and disembarked, the king and queen presented their hands to all of us, every one, with singular kindness; and so we were to get up on horseback.

Here I wish to kindly entreat the reader not to interpret the following narration as any vain glory or pride of mine, but to credit me this much, that if there had not been a special necessity for it, I could very well have utterly concealed this honour which was shown me. We were all one after another distributed amongst the lords. But our old lord, and I, most unworthy, were to ride alongside the king, each of us bearing a snow-white ensign with a red cross. Indeed, I was made use of because of my age, for we both had long grey beards and hair. I had also fastened my tokens about my hat, which the young king soon noticed, and asked if I were he who could redeem these tokens at the gate?

I answered in most humble manner, "Yes."

But he laughed at me, saying, there was no need for ceremony; I was *his* father.

Then he asked me with what I had redeemed them.

I replied, "With water and salt."

Whereupon he wondered who had made me so wise; upon which I grew a bit more confident, and recounted to him how it had happened with my bread, the dove and the raven, and he was pleased with it and said expressly that it must be that God had herein vouchsafed me a singular happiness.

With this we came to the first gate where the porter with the blue clothes waited, bearing in his hand a supplication. Now as soon as he saw me alongside the king, he delivered me the supplication, most humbly beseeching me to mention his ingenuity to the king. Now in the first place I asked the king what the condition of this porter was. He kindly answered me, that he was a very famous and rare astrologer, and always in high regard with the lord his father, but having once committed a fault against Venus, and seen her in her bed of rest, this punishment was therefore imposed upon him, that he should wait at the first gate for so long until someone should release him from it.

I replied, "May he then be released?"

"Yes," said the king, "if anyone can be found that has transgressed as highly as himself, he must take his place, and the other shall be free."

This went to my heart, for my conscience convinced me that I was the offender, yet I kept quiet, and herewith delivered the supplication. As soon as he had read it, he was greatly terrified, so that the queen (who with our virgins, and that other duchess as well – whom I mentioned at the hanging of the weights – rode just behind us) observed this, and therefore asked him what this letter might mean. But he had no mind to take any notice of it, and putting away the paper, began to talk about other matters, till thus in about three hours' time we came to the castle, where we alighted, and waited upon the king as he went into his hall.

Immediately the king called for the old Atlas to come to him in a little closet, and showed him the writing, and Atlas did not tarry, but rode out again to the porter to get more information on the matter. After this the young king, with his spouse, and the other lords, ladies and virgins, sat down. Then our virgin began to highly commend the diligence we had shown, and the pains and labour we had undergone, requesting that we might be royally rewarded, and that she might be permitted to enjoy the benefit of her commission from then on. Then the old lord stood up too, and attested that all the virgin had said was true, and that it was only just that we should both be contented on both our parts. Hereupon we were to step forward a little, and it was concluded that each man should make some possible wish, and accordingly obtain it; for it was not to be doubted that those of understanding would also make the best wish. So we were to consider it until after supper.

Meantime the king and queen, for recreation's sake, began to play together, at something which looked not unlike chess, only it had different rules; for it was the virtues and vices one against another, and it might ingeniously be observed with what plots the vices lay in wait for the virtues, and how to re-encounter them again. This was so properly and cleverly performed, that it is to be wished that we had the same game too. During the game, in came Atlas again, and made his report in private, but I blushed all over, for my conscience gave me no rest.

After this the king gave me the supplication to read, and the contents of it were much to this purpose. First he (the doorkeeper) wished the king prosperity, and increase, and that his seed might be spread abroad far and wide. Afterwards he remonstrated that the time was now come in which according to the royal promise he ought to be released, because Venus had already been uncovered by one of his guests, for his observations could not lie to him. And that if his majesty would be pleased to make a strict and diligent enquiry, he would find that she had been uncovered, and if this should not prove to be so, he would be content to remain before the gate all the days of his life. Then he asked in the most humble manner, that upon peril of body and life he might be permitted to be present at this night's supper. He was hoping to seek out the very offender, and obtain his desired freedom. This was expressly and handsomely indicated, by which I could well perceive his ingenuity, but it was too sharp for me, and I would not have minded if I had never seen it. Now I was wondering whether he might perhaps be helped through my wish, so I asked the king whether he might not be released some other way.

"No," replied the king, "because there is a special consideration in the business. However, for this night, we may well gratify him in his desire."

So he sent someone to fetch him in. Meanwhile the tables were prepared in a spacious room, in which we had never been before, which was so perfect, and contrived in such a manner, that it is not possible for me even to begin to describe it. We were conducted into this with singular pomp and ceremony. Cupid was not at this time present, for (as I was informed) the disgrace which had happened to his mother had somewhat angered him. In brief, my offence, and the supplication which was delivered, were an occasion of much sadness, for the king was in perplexity how to make inquisition amongst his guests, and the more so because through this, even they who were yet ignorant of the matter would come to know about it. So he caused the porter himself, who had already arrived, to make his strict survey, and he himself acted as pleasantly as he was able.

However, eventually they all began to be merry again, and to talk to one another with all sorts of recreational and profitable discourses. Now, how the treatment and other ceremonies were then performed, it is not necessary to declare, since it is neither the reader's concern, nor serviceable to my design. But all exceeded more in art, and human invention, than we exceeded in drinking! And this was the last and noblest meal at which I was present. After the banquet the tables were suddenly taken away, and certain curious chairs placed round about in a circle, in which we, together with the king and queen, and both their old men and the ladies and virgins, were to sit.

After this, a very handsome page opened the above-mentioned glorious little book, and Atlas immediately placed himself in the midst, and began to speak to this purpose: that his royal majesty had not forgotten the service we had done him, and how carefully we had attended to our duty, and therefore by way of retribution had elected all and each of us Knights of the Golden Stone. And that it was therefore further necessary not only once again to oblige ourselves towards his royal majesty, but also to vow to the following articles; and then his royal majesty would likewise know how to behave himself towards his liege people. Upon which he caused the page to read over the articles, which were these.

(1) You my lords the knights shall swear that you shall at no time ascribe your order to any devil or spirit, but only to God your Creator, and his handmaid Nature.

(2) That you will abominate all whoredom, incontinency and uncleanness, and not defile your order with such vices.

(3) That you through your talents will be ready to assist all that are worthy, and have need of them.

(4) That you desire not to employ this honour to worldly pride and high authority.

(5) That you shall not be willing to live longer than God will have you do.

At this last article we could not choose but laugh, and it may well have been placed after the rest only for a conceit. Now after vowing to them all by the king's sceptre, we were afterwards installed knights with the usual ceremonies, and amongst other privileges set over ignorance, poverty, and sickness, to handle them at our pleasure. And this was afterwards ratified in a little chapel (to which we were conducted in procession) and thanks returned to God for it. I also hung up there at that time my golden fleece and hat, and left them there for an eternal memorial, to the honour of God. And because everyone had to write his name there, I wrote thus:

> The highest wisdom is to know nothing.
> Brother Christian Rosenkreutz
> Knight of the Golden Stone
> A.D. 1459.

Others wrote likewise, each as it seemed good to him. After this, we were again brought into the hall, where, having sat down, we were admonished quickly to think what we each one would wish. But the king and his party retired into a little closet, there to give audience to our wishes. Now each man was called in separately, so that I cannot speak of any man's own wish. I thought nothing could be more praiseworthy than to demonstrate some laudable virtue in honour of my order, and found too that none at present could be better, and cost me more trouble, than gratitude. Wherefore in spite of the fact that I might well have wished something more dear and agreeable to myself, I vanquished myself, and concluded, even at my own peril, to free the porter, my benefactor.

So as I was now called in, I was first of all asked whether, having read the supplication, I had observed or suspected nothing concerning the offender? Upon which I began undauntedly to relate how all the business had passed, how through ignorance I fell into that mistake, and so offered myself to undergo all that I had thereby deserved. The king, and the rest of the lords, wondered greatly at so unexpected a confession, and so asked me to step aside a little.

Now as soon as I was called in again, Atlas declared to me that although it was grievous to the king's majesty that I, whom he loved above others, had fallen into such a mischance, yet because it was not possible for him to transgress his ancient usages, he did not know how to absolve me; the other must be at liberty, and I put in his place; yet he would hope that some other would be apprehended, so that I might be able to go home again. However, no release was to be hoped for, till the marriage feast of his future son.

This sentence had nearly cost me my life, and I first hated myself and my twaddling tongue, in that I could not keep quiet; yet at last I took courage, and because I thought there was no remedy, I related how this porter had bestowed a token on me, and commended me to the other, by whose assistance I stood upon the scale, and so was made partaker of all the honour and joy already received. And therefore now it was but fair that I should show myself grateful to my benefactor, and because this could not be done in any other way, I returned thanks for the sentence, and was willing gladly to bear some inconvenience for the sake of he who had been helpful to me in coming to such a high place. But if by my wish anything might be effected, I wished myself at home again, so that he by me, and I by my wish might be at liberty. Answer was made me, that the wishing did not stretch so far. However, I might wish him free. Yet it was very pleasing to his royal majesty that I had behaved myself so generously in this, but he was afraid I might still be ignorant of what a miserable condition I had plunged myself into through my curiosity. Hereupon the good man was pronounced free, and I with a sad heart had to step aside.

After me the rest were called for too, and came jocundly out again, which pained me still more, for I imagined nothing other than that I must finish my life under the gate. I also had many pensive thoughts running up and down in my head, what I should do, and how to spend the time. At length I considered that I was now old, and according to the course of nature, had few years more to live. And that this anguished and melancholy life would quickly send me from this world, and then my door-keeping would be at an end, and by a most happy sleep I might quickly bring myself to the grave. I had many of these thoughts. Sometimes it vexed me that I had seen such gallant things, and must be robbed of them. Sometimes I rejoiced that still, before my end, I had been accepted to all joy, and should not be forced to depart shamefully. This was the last and worst shock that I sustained.

During my cogitations the rest had got ready. So after they had received a good night from the king and lords, each one was conducted into his lodging. But I, most wretched man, had nobody to show me the way, and must moreover suffer myself to be tormented; and so that I might be certain of my future function, I had to put on the ring which the other had worn before. Finally, the king exhorted me that since this was now the last time I was likely to see him in this manner, I should behave myself according to my place, and not against the order. Upon which he took me in his arms, and kissed me, all which I understood to mean that in the morning I must sit at my gate. Now after they had all spoken in a friendly manner to me for a while, and at last given their hands, committing me to the divine protection, I was conducted by both the old men, the lord of the tower, and Atlas, into a glorious lodging, in which stood three beds, and each of us lay in one of them, where we spent almost two, &c ...

Here about two leaves in quarto are missing, and he (the author of this), whereas he imagined he must in the morning be doorkeeper, returned home.

The Seventh Day: Commentary

When one becomes deeply immersed in the content of the *Chymical Wedding*, sooner or later the question arises: What does this tell me? What have I to do with this great story? Am I supposed to read it just like a fairytale or fantastic invention? And what if it really describes the imaginations of an initiation? That is exactly when one can look up to this story as to a gigantic mountain – beautiful to look at, but not to climb it. And yet, the answers to the question – what does this tell me? – are not hard to find. If we have not recognised this in the foregoing, we certainly will in the events of the last day.

The crucial motif of alchemists and Rosicrucians is love for the earth, but in an exceptional manner. We know this love in its crude, uncultivated form, when we enjoy nature and become attached to places and things and people. We are all familiar with the contradictory activities we develop in our connection with the earth. The philosopher Pascal (1623–62) begins one of the fragments in his *Pensées* (thoughts) with the words: "The sinners lick the dust." (No. 665). When we surrender to the earth and lose ourselves in it we enter into an impure relationship with it, a corrupted love that reigns supreme in materialism: earth craving. We also see the opposite in countless people who want nothing more to do with the earth and its misery: flight from the earth. And here, in the *Chymical Wedding*, we have a middle way that creates a spiritually real relationship with the earth, a Christian way through and through.

We can arrive at that insight with the aid of three concepts from Goethe's book *Wilhelm Meister's Apprenticeship*. More than once in his life, Goethe received Rosicrucian inspirations; examples are *The Fairytale of the Green Snake and the Beautiful Lily* and the poem *The Mysteries*. In *Wilhelm Meister* he distinguishes three forms of religion, three "love relationships" with the divine world. The oldest religious form is that of love for the divine world *above* us. Our church-oriented forms of Christianity are still largely determined by this form of love, a form to which young children cannot easily relate. For children want to connect with the earth; they have just come from above! A pious mother who, with the best of intentions, said the following prayer with her child: "Dear God, make me devout so that I will go to heaven," upon which the child burst into tears and said,

"I don't want to go to heaven. I want to be on the earth!" We often imagine religion in this way; not that it is bad, but it is one-sided, as the above anecdote shows. Goethe calls this the Old Testament form of religion, the worship of the Father God.

He also describes a love that directs itself to the world *beside* us, our fellow human beings. This is where religion begins to be Christian. We also know this form from traditional Christianity.

Goethe calls a third form of religion the love we have for what is *under* us. "How difficult is it to not only let the earth lie beneath us and pride ourselves on a higher place of birth, but to accept humility and poverty, mockery and disdain, indignity and misery, suffering and death, and acknowledge them as divine! Yes, and to view even sin and crime not as obstacles, but to venerate and love them as an appeal to the sacred!" That, says Goethe, is the highest, partly future form of religion which raises what is beneath us to humanness and godliness.

In my view, that is the Christian form of the *Chymical Wedding*. We can practise this every day, especially in a world like ours, in such a way that in the manner we deal with the world that lies beneath us we make our religious forces available to the suffering earth, the suffering animal realm, and human suffering. Thus we can begin, perhaps clumsily and on a tiny scale, to bring something into balance of what we have done to the earth in the course of the centuries.

We will see this once more, namely when the highest has been achieved and Christian Rosenkreutz and his companions have become Knights of the Golden Stone, and have been confirmed as such by the king.

Once when Rudolf Steiner spoke of the personality of Christian Rosenkreutz and his task he used a shocking expression. Steiner was not liberal with superlatives. When he did use them we know that he was talking about something quite extraordinary. Thus in one of his lectures he called Christian Rosenkreutz a "noble martyr whose manner of working asked, and will continue to ask, more endurance of him than of any other human being. I say 'human being,' for what Christ suffered was suffered by a God."[1] The highest one also bears what is lowest, heaviest, most difficult. A historic example of a phase on this path of suffering is without any doubt the mockery, the denunciations as heresy, the insinuations and outright combat against the Rosicrucians of the seventeenth century, as outlined in the Introduction to this book.

The seventh day begins with the golden fleece, the token of initiation, and the appointment of the companions as Knights of the Golden Stone, at which time they each receive a gold medal. As Jason captured the golden fleece after an succession of trials, so the initiates receive the same token after having survived a dangerous journey. Only now are the black habits exchanged for yellow ones.

We can recognise in this initiation four steps that have been known from olden times:

1. Christian Rosenkreutz receives the invitation to the wedding from the angel;
2. He offers up a number of belongings: bread, water, salt and cloak;
3. He goes through a series of transformations – the seven alchemical phases;
4. He unites himself with the spiritual world – the chymical wedding; king and queen.

These are the same phases that we are familiar with in the Christian Eucharist: Gospel Reading, Offertory, Transubstantiation and Communion.

The following verse by the mystic Angelus Silesius helps us understand the nature of the Golden Stone:

> Your stone, alchemist, is nothing,
> The cornerstone which I mean
> Is my gold tincture*
> Is the stone of all wise men.
>
> *Dein Stein, Chemist, ist nichts,*
> *Der Eckstein den ich mein'*
> *ist meine Goldtinktur*
> *ist aller Weisen Stein.*[2]

---

* "Tincture" is the end product of the alchemical process.

Again, the verse points out that the "stone" of the false alchemists, gold, has no meaning. What is the Golden Stone that has to be found? It is the cornerstone, the stone of the true gold, the Philosopher's Stone. "...the stone which the builders have called useless – the main cornerstone, that is to say the stumbling-block and the rock which causes them to fall" (1Pet.2:7f M).

In his work *De Incarnatione Verbi* (the incarnation of the word), Jakob Böhme, who more than once uses alchemical expressions in his writings, addresses the alchemists of his time as follows: "Let this be clear to you, seekers for the tincture: if you want to find the Philosopher's Stone, then bring yourself to birth anew in Christ."

In the catharsis, development and transformations which the alchemist went through, the physical body became the Philosopher's Stone, Christ's dwelling place. The decisive question for the Rosicrucians was: how does Christianity become flesh and blood?

How can we imagine that the risen Christ makes his home in the physical body? If we intensively practice Christian meditation and prayer for a time, we may notice that our breathing changes. Unwittingly, a person who meditates intensively breathes more deeply. And the blood also changes. We may often be swept along in furious rage or icy hatred. This changes when we begin to lead a meditative life: what turns our blood hot or cold disappears, and allows the real human middle to open up. We can experience this even in physical warmth.

The body of individuals who intensively school themselves in spiritual practice, is transformed even in its physiognomy. It is possible to recognise in their countenance whether they live with meditation or prayer. In the portrait of the poet Novalis, for instance, one can see how the eyes and the exceptional complexion are expressions of the spiritualisation of the body. A Christian – and this is especially true for the Christianity of Christian Rosenkreutz – is someone in whom Christ begins to "incarnate," in such a way that it becomes visible even in the body. Something of the future human being then becomes visible, the new Adam which, in the words of St Paul, one "puts on" as one can put on a garment. In this connection the description, given on the sixth day, of the appearance and clothing of the king and queen is significant.

The two inscriptions on the gold medal are to be found in the margin of the original edition of the *Chymical Wedding*: *Ars naturae ministra* (Art is the priestess or servant of nature) and *Temporis natura filia* (Nature is the daughter of time). It was certainly the mission of alchemy (here called "Art") to continue nature, but nature was never to be upset or overpowered by the human being. One could say that the quintessence of this level of development, inscribed on the gold medal, is: Never go against nature; never go against what is favoured by time, by the moment. In previous chapters we have seen that time – in the form of conjunctions of planets – played a decisive role. Something new could be created on earth because the cosmos made it possible. In this connection, Rudolf Steiner wrote about the seventh day:

> What Christian Rosenkreutz and his associates accomplish
> in external life will flow from the spirit from which nature's
> own works flow. Through their work they will bring harmony
> into human life that will depict the harmony of nature that
> is capable of conquering disharmony. The presence of such
> people in the social order is a continuously effective impulse
> toward a healthy way of life.[3]

Time and again, when we are reading the *Chymical Wedding*, we are confronted with surprises that make us think. The seven ships on which the group travelled to Olympus Tower turn into twelve for the return trip. In countless cultures, seven is the expression of time. This is obviously reflected in the seven days of the week. When those days have passed, a time span is completed. While the seven planets are the expression of time, the twelve constellations of the zodiac with its fixed stars is more an expression of space.

There is an impressive moment when the "seven" become "twelve" in Wagner's opera *Parsifal*, when Parsifal enters the Grail Castle for the first time, and thereby enters into a spiritual reality. *Totaliter aliter,* our medieval monks would have said. Everything changes around him so that he wonders what he is actually seeing. And the answer of the Grail Knight Gurnemanz is, "You see, my son, here time becomes space." When we enter into the spiritual world, time ceases to exist and turns into space around us. We know the phenomenon in our time from experiences at the threshold of death: our entire life becomes a spatial panorama, a tableau all around us.

Although at this moment in the *Chymical Wedding* the path leads back to the earth, the initiates, the old wise man, the virgin, the king and queen bring with them the fruit of the initiation.

In the meantime, the four great initiates and their companions have come together again. On the way back they are all travelling in one ship. True Rosicrucians will never pride themselves on their special capacities in order to leave others behind. On the contrary, from the beginning Rosicrucians have tried to bring new forms into the social life of all layers of the population. The seed for this work was planted already in the *Fama,* in which Christian Rosenkreutz speaks of a "society" that unites all spiritual science and wisdom of its time in order to give a new impulse to social life, free of politics and Church. This original social idea was taken up by several people in the seventeenth century. In 1620, Andreae and a group of like-minded individuals attempted to found a "Christian Society," but the Thirty Years War made the initiative impossible. Karl Heyer gives a detailed description of the further historical development, which ends in the devaluation of the original idea and its perversion in the Royal Society in England.[4]

The twelve ships are flying banners with the signs of the zodiac; Christian Rosenkreutz's ship has the banner with Libra, the scales. The golden mean, balance between extremes, is a motif that accompanies the *Chymical Wedding* from beginning to end. It is announced on the first day already in the invitation to the wedding, in the Rebis sign: sun and moon, king and queen, heaven and earth come together in this alchemical symbol. We will continue to meet this theme of balance or middle until the end of the story. Christian Rosenkreutz relates with some emphasis that there was on board "a noble and curious clock, which showed us all the minutes." It is a confirmation of the inscription on the gold medal: nature is the daughter of time.

One person who is also travelling in Christian Rosenkreutz's ship is the wise old man, the messenger of a timeless world: "he knew so well how to pass away our time with wonderful stories, that I could have been content to sail with him all my life long." The clock, however, reminds them of the earthly reality that is coming back to them. After they arrived at the lake, which is connected to the great sea by a channel, a large fleet comes to meet them with the king and queen on board one of its ships. Only now do the gold makers, who had laboured on the seventh storey, see with astonishment the results of the "great work." "The rest of my companions were in great amazement, where this king should come from, for they imagined nothing other than that they would have to awaken him again. We allowed them to continue in their amazement, and acted as if it seemed strange to us too." To greet the king, two persons representing two very different worlds speak to him: Atlas and the wise old man. In Greek mythology, Atlas is the Titan's son who has to carry the vault of heaven on his shoulders. He was pictured as the epitome of strength. By contrast, the wise old man lets the light of his consciousness shine on things. And between the two, between the primal power of will and the primal power of wisdom, stands the third, Christian Rosenkreutz, who has brought to completion the forces of the heart.

This search for the middle between extremes can also be recognised in the historical context in which the Rosicrucians appeared. It is no coincidence that the work of the Rosicrucians appeared in a time when the outer world was being explored as never before. The Rosicrucians created this necessary connection with the physical world without, however, breaking the bond with the spiritual world. Only if human beings remain true to both worlds can they fulfil their destiny.

After the width of the sea of life, the earthly world gradually comes into view again. They land close to the gate where Christian Rosenkreutz first gained entry into the world of spirit. Here we are for the first time introduced to animals that pre-eminently belong to our earthly reality: horses. In cultural history we recognise horses as animals that have a connection with human intelligence; horses played an important role in Greek culture. The Book of Revelation describes the white, red, black and pale horses as cosmic intelligence becoming earthly and human intelligence (Rev.6). Here Christian Rosenkreutz comes close to the portal that separates, but also connects, the two worlds. And the first thing which, from the other side, becomes recognisable as earthly reality bordering on the spiritual, is the world of thinking.

Because Christian Rosenkreutz is one of the oldest, he, together with the old man, rides next to the king. The king notices that he wears the guest tokens. "[He] asked if I were he who could redeem these tokens at the gate? I answered in most humble manner, 'Yes'." And now comes a surprising turn in the conversation: "he laughed at me, saying, there was no need for ceremony; I was *his* father."

This shows how deeply the parable reaches: he has begotten this king. When the egg was produced, the relation of the alchemists to this creature was still expressed in a comparison: "We stood round about this egg as jocund as if we ourselves had laid it." At the bloody wedding also it still sounded like a parable: "the life of these now stands in your hands, and if you follow me, this death shall make many alive."

Now Christian Rosenkreutz is the creator of this royal being; he is the king's father.* They come to the first portal, where the guardian with the blue cloak was standing, who was the first to welcome Christian Rosenkreutz to this realm. Now follows a long, enigmatic passage:

> With this we came to the first gate where the porter with the blue clothes waited, bearing in his hand a supplication. Now as soon as he saw me alongside the king, he delivered me the supplication, most humbly beseeching me to mention his ingenuity to the king. Now in the first place I asked the king what the condition of this porter was. He kindly answered me, that he was a very famous and rare astrologer, and always in high regard with the lord his father, but having once committed a fault against Venus, and seen her in her bed of rest, this punishment was therefore imposed upon him, that he should wait at the first gate for so long until someone should release him from it.
>
> I replied, "May he then be released?"
>
> "Yes," said the king, "if anyone can be found that has transgressed as highly as himself, he must take his place, and the other shall be free."
>
> This went to my heart, for my conscience convinced me that I was the offender, yet I kept quiet, and herewith delivered the supplication.

---

* This title, Father, was the seventh and highest grade in the ancient Persian initiation.

What is going on between these two? The porter and Christian Rosenkreutz have a certain relationship with each other. On day two this porter let him pass with the words: "Go ahead, my brother; you are my welcome guest!" Both of them have gazed on Venus. No doubt, as an astrologer, the porter knows about this; and no doubt his petition refers to this. Is it such a serious misdeed that Christian Rosenkreutz has gazed on Venus? It is a riddle to him, and his conscience gives him no peace.

Each of the Knights of the Golden Stone may make a wish which will be fulfilled. It is permitted at this stage, because they will now only wish what also is necessary. But now Christian Rosenkreutz is again subjected to a great temptation. When he reads the petition of the porter, who has indeed perceived that Venus had been disclosed to one of the guests, he is willing to free the porter, but not to take his place. But this is an impossibility for the king. There has to be a guardian at the portal. In actual fact, he asked something that runs counter to the laws of the spiritual world, to the rules of the last medal.

All of them are now confirmed as Knights of the Golden Stone. They have to observe five rules:

1. Everything Rosicrucians do is *soli Deo Gloria,* only to the honour of God and his nature.
2. "You will abominate all whoredom, incontinency and uncleanness, and not defile your order with such vices."
3. "Through your talents will be ready to assist all that are worthy, and have need of them."
4. "You desire not to employ this honour to worldly pride and high authority."

One reason why we know so little of the true Rosicrucians is that they at all times had to work in secret. There even was a very strict rule in their movement that Christian Rosenkreutz must not be mentioned for one hundred years.[5] The last rule is:

5. "You shall not be willing to live longer than God will have you do."

At this last rule the Knights of the Golden Stone have to laugh heartily. After all, in the state they have now developed this has become obvious. They have taken into their own conscious will even the seeming arbitrariness and fickleness of destiny. Great initiates are capable under all circumstances to act in accordance with their own insight and judgment. That becomes possible when one is able to say at all times and in all circumstances: "not my will, but thine, be done" (Lk.22:42).

Christian Rosenkreutz leaves behind some of what he had further received on his path of initiation: "[we gave] thanks ... to God for it. I also hung up there at that time my golden fleece and hat, and left them there for an eternal memorial, to the honour of God." The golden fleece, symbol of the newly acquired ether body, is from that moment no longer his "property," but is available to all who want to connect with his impulses.

Above his name – and this is the one and only time that his name is mentioned in full – Christian Rosenkreutz sums up what he has gained at his initiation: the highest wisdom is to know nothing. The highest form of spiritual wisdom is no longer to know with the earthly intellect but with another capacity. I am reminded here of the words of a wise human being, the founder of Camphill, Karl König, who had a remarkable capacity of "thinking with the heart." He would say, "Each *genuine* question opens a portal to the spiritual world. Most of the answers we give close the portal ..." That is how I picture the highest wisdom!

Christian Rosenkreutz goes through a profound temptation. At first sight it looks as if he will be unable to accomplish what is needed. Even at this stage, the very last moment, the opposing powers still continue in their role. "Wherefore in spite of the fact that I might well have wished something more dear and agreeable to myself, I vanquished myself, and concluded, even at my own peril, to free the porter, my benefactor."*

In the end, his action proceeds out of his own free will and insight, and he chooses the most difficult thing a person can be confronted with at this stage of the path of initiation. "[I] offered

---

* Christian Rosenkreutz calls him a benefactor because the porter had given him the first token and thus had recommended him to the others. He even says that thanks to the help of the two porters he was able to survive the weighing.

myself to undergo all that I had thereby deserved …This sentence had nearly cost me my life …Yet it was very pleasing to his royal majesty that I had behaved myself so generously in this …"

Now that he has made his decision, the temptations really converge on him. We know it – when at the end of life a person begins to have doubts from the bottom of his heart: Has everything I have done been for naught? I wish I was never born! The original edition of the *Chymical Wedding* has a note in the margin: "Author is troubled."

Christian Rosenkreutz has to withstand two temptations. The first is despair: what has been the sense of it all? "This anguished and melancholy life would quickly send me from this world, and then my door-keeping would be at an end." The other temptation is flight from reality: "by a most happy sleep I might quickly bring myself to the grave." Again, what happened between him and the gatekeeper so that he has to take the latter's place? Did he indeed incur guilt?

In the life of the spirit – where we continue to sojourn at this stage of the story – life is not subdivided into pigeon holes. Whether we know it or not, everything is connected with everything. The situation is such that one has to say: Christian Rosenkreutz is not alone with himself. The porter is part of him. He represents that part of the human being that stands at the threshold of the spiritual world and has to experience the tragedy of having to remain outside: our double.

In the words of Rudolf Steiner:

Christian Rosenkreutz's relationship to the "First Gatekeeper" is really a relationship to part of his own being – in other words, a relationship to that part of his being which as "Astrologer" searched for the laws determining human life but was unable (before the transformation of his cognitive powers) to face a temptation like the one at the beginning of the fifth day when Christian Rosenkreutz confronted Venus. Those who succumb to this temptation cannot gain entrance to the spiritual world. They know too much to be entirely shut away from it, but they cannot enter. They must stand guard before the door until another appears and falls victim to the same temptation.

Christian Rosenkreutz supposes himself to have succumbed

and thus to have been condemned to take over "The Office of Watchman." But this watchman is part of himself, and because he can survey it with his other, transformed part, he is able to overcome it. *He becomes the watchman of his own soul life.* [emphasis added][6]

This is the highest form of development: when a human being releases the double from his thankless task. Christian Rosenkreutz has to put the ring of the porter on his finger; he is "bound," and must from now on experience what otherwise the double has to go through.

The end of the story presents another riddle:

Finally, the king exhorted me that since this was now the last time I was likely to see him in this manner, I should behave myself according to my place, and not against the order. Upon which he took me in his arms, and kissed me, all which I understood to mean that in the morning I must sit at my gate. Now after they had all spoken in a friendly manner to me for a while, and at last given their hands, committing me to the divine protection, I was conducted by both the old men, the lord of the tower, and Atlas, into a glorious lodging, in which stood three beds, and each of us lay in one of them, where we spent almost two, &c ...

Three beds, for Atlas, Christian Rosenkreutz and the wise old man. Primal strength, primal wisdom, and between the two the human being who brings love to realisation. Not only can this human being be found and recognised since then in the realm of spirit; the great initiates can be in more than one place at the same time. Not only does he stand at the threshold as guardian; he also lives unknown, often reviled and persecuted, as an initiate among human beings. Tradition has it that Christian Rosenkreutz incarnates on earth again in each century.[7]

Who is Christian Rosenkreutz?

In the spiritual tradition of the West we can find a number of references to incarnations of Christian Rosenkreutz. I want to mention only one of these, because he could then be found in the immediate circle around Christ. At times, Rudolf Steiner spoke of his incarnation as one of the twelve disciples, saying that Christian Rosenkreutz is the same as the one who, in the remarkable words of the Gospel, has experienced the love of the Lord.[1] (see Jn.21:20) This is not a statement we need to accept without further ado, but we can make an effort to understand why Steiner focuses here on St John the Evangelist. In the earliest days of Christianity John has a special place, not only metaphorically but also literally. The Greek text of the Gospel of St John has two words for John's place with Christ. A literal translation of John 13:23–25 would be as follows:

> One of his disciples was reclining in the lap [*kolpos*] of Jesus, whom Jesus loved. So Simon Peter beckoned to him and said, "Ask who it is of whom he speaks." He, falling back on the breast [*stēthos*] of Jesus, says to him: Lord, who is it?

The Greek word *kolpos,* lap, also indicates a profound spiritual connection between two persons. St John uses the same word in his Prologue to describe the bond between the Son and the Father (Jn.1:18). As the Son relates to the Father, so John relates to Christ. When John raises himself from the lap to the breast this indicates that his deep connection of will raises itself to awareness in the realm of feeling, the region of the heart. He asks him the crucial question: Lord, who is it who will betray you? He is the disciple who is so deeply connected with Jesus that he can hear in Jesus' heart what is not to be found in any of the other gospels.

Tradition relates that, when many years later he dictates the opening words of his gospel to his scribe, the latter falls as if dead at the feet of John, overwhelmed by the power of the words of the Prologue. Whoever immerses himself for a long time in the original Greek text of this Prologue, may begin to have an inkling of the mantric power hidden in these words.

To this day we can visit the cave on the island of Patmos where John lived for a number of years. It is as if we get a preview here of the crucial alchemical motif of the interior of the earth. Legend tells that he had to work in the mines of Patmos. The imagination developed: When John took a stone in his hands it turned into a precious stone. The creation changes in the hands of this great Christian initiate. So it is no coincidence that the Rosicrucians gave him the name, John the Alchemist. The motif of the deep connection with the heart of Jesus returns in a powerful image in the life story of Christian Rosenkreutz, as told by Valentin Andreae in the *Fama*. When after 120 years the tomb of Christian Rosenkreutz is rediscovered by his followers, they find a booklet in the hands of the deceased, in which is written: *Christian Rosenkreutz: granum pectori Jesu insitum,* "a kernel of grain planted in the heart of Jesus."

What in the incarnation of John the Disciple, the first Christian initiate, was realised as a relation of *agape* (selfless, spiritual love) to Jesus, is developed further in the incarnation of Christian Rosenkreutz, who has the deepest possible relation to the Saviour: *in* the heart of Jesus.

Notes

Introduction

1 "On the *Chymical Wedding* of Christian Rosenkreutz," originally written for the journal *Das Reich*, 1917–18, included in Steiner, *Philosophie und Anthroposophie;* English in Steiner, *The Secret Stream.*

The Title Page

1 Steiner, *The Secret Stream,* pp. 165.

The First Day

1 From Polzer-Hoditz, *Memories of Rudolf Steiner.*
2 Villanova, *Drey unterschiedliche Tractate von der Alchimey.* Original text: *dass unser Magisterium anders nichts sey / als Mann und Weib / und desselben Zusammenfügung.*

The Second Day

1 Allen, *A Christian Rosenkreutz Anthology,* page 175.
2 Steiner, *The Secret Stream,* p. 188.
3 Richard van Dülmen indicates that the four ways are already to be found in the works of Mani and Hermes Trismegistus. See his book *Johann Valentin Andreae.*
4 Described in detail in Meyer, *Elias,* pp. 74–76.

The Third Day

1 Rudolf Steiner, *How to Know Higher Worlds,* p. 62.
2 Steiner, *The Secret Stream,* p. 173.
3 Steiner, *The Secret Stream,* p. 178.
4 See Dülmen, *Johann Valentin Andreae.* He calls the first four maidens the cardinal virtues: courage, prudence, temperance and justice.

The Fourth Day

1 Steiner, *Truth-Wrought Words,* p. 15. The original German verse is:
   Dem Stoff sich verschreiben
   Heisst Seelen zerreiben.
   Im Geiste sich finden
   Heisst Menschen verbinden.
   In Menschen sich schauen
   Heisst Welten erbauen.

2 Quoted in Anonymous, *Meditations on the Tarot.*
3 CVH, *Einfältige und kurze Antwort über die ausgegangene Fama.*
4 Steiner, *The Secret Stream,* p. 185.
5 See also Steiner, *Esoteric Christianity,* lecture of Sep 28, 1911.
6 See for instance Beckh, *Alchymie,* for the connection between alchemy and the New Jerusalem from the Book of Revelation.
7 See Steiner, *How to Know Higher Worlds,* Chapter 9, "The Splitting of the Personality in Esoteric Training".

The Fifth Day

1 See Steiner, *An Outline of Esoteric Science,* Chapter 6.
2 Steiner, *The Secret Stream,* pp. 163f.
3 Steiner, *The Secret Stream,* p. 177.
4 Translation Philip Mees

The Sixth Day

1 For an extensive description of the seven phases see Kossmann, *Alchemie und Mystik.*
2 Maier, *Chymisches Cabinet.*
3 Levi, *Transcendental Magic: its Dogma and Ritual,* Part II.

The Seventh Day

1 Steiner, *Esoteric Christianity and the Mission of Christian Rosenkreutz,* p. 279, lecture of June 17, 1912.
2 Transl. Philip Mees from *Der Cherubinische Wandersmann.*
3 Steiner, *The Secret Stream,* pp. 187f.
4 Heyer, Karl, *Geschichtsimpulse des Rosenkreuzertum,* chapter "Der Fortgang des 17. Jahrhunderts".
5 Steiner, *Three Paths of the Soul to Christ,* April 17, 1912.
6 Steiner, *The Secret Stream,* p. 187.
7 Steiner, *Esoteric Christianity and the Mission of Christian Rosenkreutz,* lecture of Sep 27, 1911.

Who is Christian Rosenkreutz?

1 Steiner, *"Freemasonry" and Ritual Work, the Misraim Service,* p.431.

Bibliography

Adams, George, *Christ in the Power of Memory and the Power of Love,* London 1938 [a description of the Rosicrucian movement and its relation to great initiates, Zarathustra, Buddha, Skythianos, and Manes].

—, *The Mysteries of the Rose Cross,* East Grinstead, UK 1955.

Allen, Paul M. *A Christian Rosenkreutz Anthology,* Rudolf Steiner Publications, USA 1968 [contains English translations of the original works by Andreae, and a collection of essays on a variety of themes relating to the Rosicrucians, such as the *Chymical Wedding,* alchemy, Karlstein, the castle of Charles IV and the connection with Rosicrucians].

Anonymous, *Meditations on the Tarot: A Journey into Christian Hermeticism,* (tr. Robert Powell), Tarcher/Putnam, USA 2002.

Beckh, Hermann, *Alchymie: Vom Geheimnis der Stoffeswelt,* Dornach 1987 [a description of alchemy and its connection with the past (Genesis, mythology), present and future (Apocalypse)].

Berk, M. F. M. van den, *The Magic Flute: an Alchemical Allegory,* Brill 2003.

Boccalini, *Allgemeine und Generalreformation der ganzen Welt,* German translation Kassel 1614.

Burckhardt, Titus, *Alchemy: Science of the Cosmos, Science of the Soul,* Fons Vitae, USA 2000.

Cimelia Rhodostaurotica. Die Rosenkreuzer im Spiegel der zwischen 1610 und 1660 erstandenen Handschriften und Drucke, Bibliotheca Philosophica Hermetica, Amsterdam 1995 [catalogue of an exhibition in the University Library Amsterdam, where 350 Rosicrucian documents were on view].

CVH, *Einfältige und kurze Antwort über die ausgegangene Fama.*

Dülmen, Richard van, *Johann Valentin Andreae, Fama Fraternitatis, Confessio Fraternitatis, Chymische Hochzeit Christiani Rosencreutz,* Stuttgart 1972 [contains the original German text of *The Chymical Wedding*].

Erbe des Christian Rosenkreutz, Das. Johann Valentin Andreae und die Manifeste des Rosenkreuzerbruderschaft, Das, lectures given at a symposium in Amsterdam, November 18–20, 1986, Bibliotheca Philosophica Hermetica, Amsterdam 1986 [historical and philosophical lectures on the Rosicrucian movement].

Heyer, Karl, *Geschichtsimpulse des Rosenkreuzertum: Aus dem Jahrhundert der französischen Revolution,* Basle 1990 [a thorough historical description of the origin, development and offshoots of the Rosicrucians].

Kienast, Richard, 'Johann Valentin Andreae und die vier echten Rosenkreutzer-Schriften,' in *Palaestra,* Leipzig 1926.

Kolisko, Lili, *Das Silber und der Mond,* Stuttgart 1929.

Kossmann, Bernhard, *Alchemie und Mystik in Johann Valentin Andreaes Chymischer Hochzeit Christiani Rosenkreutz,* dissertation, Cologne 1966 [an extensive description of the *Chymical Wedding* as a symbolic description of alchemical processes].

Levi, Eliphas, *Transcendental Magic: its Dogma and Ritual,* London (reprinted) 1958.

Maier, Michael, *Atalanta Fugiens,* 1617 (later republished as *Chymisches Cabinet,* Frankfurt 1708.

Die Manifeste der Rosenkreuzerbruderschaft, Catalogue of an exhibition in the Bibliotheca Philosophica Hermetica, Amsterdam 1986 [an overview of manifestoes and manuscripts from the sixteenth and seventeenth centuries].

Meyer, Rudolf, *Elias,* Stuttgart 1964.

—, *Der Gral und seine Hüter,* Stuttgart 2003 [the chapter about the Rose Cross contains a succinct review of the beginning of the Rosicrucian movement].

Pascal, Blaise, *Pensées* (Intr. T.S. Eliot), Dutton, USA 1958.

Peuckert, Wil-Erich, *Die Rosenkreutzer: zur Geschichte einer Reformation,* Jena 1928.

Poeppig, Fred, *Ursymbole der Menschheit unter besonderer Berücksichtigung der Rosenkreuzersymbolik,* Freiburg 1972 [contains chapters on alchemical symbols, the *Chymical Wedding,* Rosicrucian symbolism in later writings, and other subjects].

Polzer-Hoditz, Ludwig, *Memories of Rudolf Steiner,* St George/Rudolf Steiner College Publications, USA 1987.

Regenstreif, Paul (ed.) *Christian Rosenkreutz und seine Mission, Studienmaterial auf der Grundlage von Hinweisen Rudolf Steiners,* Freiburg 1977 [a collection of separate quotations from lectures by Rudolf Steiner, arranged by subject].

Roboz, Steven, *Christian Rosenkreutz from the Works of Rudolf Steiner,* Steiner Book Centre, Vancouver 1982 [a collection of quotations].

Silesius, Angelus, *Der Cherubinische Wandersmann,* Zurich 1979.

Steiner, Rudolf. Volume Nos refer to the Collected Works (CW), or to the German Gesamtausgabe (GA).

—, *Esoteric Christianity and the Mission of Christian Rosenkreutz,* CW 130, Rudolf Steiner Press 2005.

—, *"Freemasonry" and Ritual Work, the Misraim Service,* CW 265, SteinerBooks 2007.

—, *How to Know Higher Worlds,* CW 10, Anthroposophic Press 1994.

—, *An Outline of Esoteric Science,* CW 13, Anthropsophic Press, USA 1997.

—, *Philosophie und Anthroposophie: Gesammelte Aufsätze 1904–1923,* GA 35, Dornach 1984.

—, *The Secret Stream: Christian Rosenkreutz and Rosicrucianism,* Anthroposophic Press, USA 2000.

—, *Three Paths of the Soul to Christ,* Anthroposophic Press, USA 1942.

—, *Truth-Wrought Words* (transl. Arvia MacKaye Ege), Anthroposophic Press 1979.

Stracke, Viktor, *Das Geistgebäude der Rosenkreuzer,* Dornach 1993 [an effort to make the symbolism of the Rosicrucians accessible].

Villanova, Arnaldus de, *Drey unterschiedliche Tractate von der Alchimey,* Frankfurt, 1604.

Waters, Frank, *Masked Gods,* New York 1970.

Index

Ways Into
Christian Meditation

Bastiaan Baan

Meditation has long been a path to self-awareness, as well as a way of consciously building a bridge into the spiritual world. Many of the most popular techniques originated in eastern traditions, but this book describes a decades-old approach that comes from western Christianity.

The author starts by describing the steps necessary to make meditation possible, drawing on some of the ideas of Rudolf Steiner. He goes on to discuss different forms of meditation, such as 'review of the day', meditations on specific words and images, and meditations for the deceased.

Finally he describes a specifically Christian approach, with a few words and sentences from the Gospel of St John leading to several fruitful subjects for meditation.

This is a deep, insightful book from an experienced priest.

florisbooks.co.uk

Old and New Mysteries

From Trials to Initiation

Bastiaan Baan

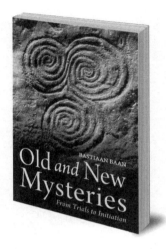

There is great contemporary interest in the mystery centres of antiquity, such as prehistoric caves, the pyramids of Egypt, Newgrange in Ireland, and the Externsteine in Germany. The trials and rites that took place there were for the chosen few, and are vividly described in this book – from the trials of fire and water to the three-day near-death sleep.

The author goes on to argue that modern-day initiation, however, has a substantially different character. Whereas a 'hierophant' – a guide – was previously needed to navigate a trial, these days it is life itself which brings us trials, which can sometimes lead to deeper experiences of the spiritual. between Christianity and the natural world.

florisbooks.co.uk

Lord of the Elements

Interweaving Christianity and Nature

Bastiaan Baan

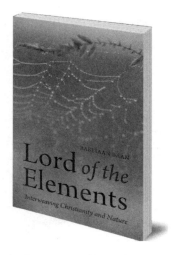

The four classical elements of earth, water, air and fire are present in Genesis and continue to be significant throughout Christianity. Different streams of thought, such as the School of Chartres, and Celtic Christianity, have emphasised the elements in different ways.

In this unique book, Bastiaan Baan, an experienced spiritual thinker, brings these elements together with ideas from Rudolf Steiner's anthroposophy. He considers, in particular, how elemental beings – nature spirits – relate to the four elements, and explores the role of elemental beings in our world.

This is a fascinating and original work on the connections between Christianity and the natural world.

 Also available as an eBook

florisbooks.co.uk

Nature Contemplations Through the Christian Year

Peter Skaller

This little book is a treasure trove of reflections and contemplations on images from nature, each one connected to a gospel reading.

Based on thirty years of sermons, Skaller explores the essence of sensory images such as flowers, shells, clouds and landscapes, going deeper to help us understand them as divine manifestations in our everyday world. They in turn enable us to come to insights, feelings and intuitions about the purpose of the world, and of ourselves.

Presented in a beautiful gift hardback edition, this is a book of reverence and wonder, in which we can glimpse the reality of the divine.

florisbooks.co.uk

Floris
Books

For news on all our **latest books,**
and to receive **exclusive discounts,**
join our mailing list at:

florisbooks.co.uk

Plus subscribers get a FREE book
with every online order!